ALBUM COVERS FROM **THE VINYL JUNKYARD**
BOOTH-CLIBBORN EDITIONS HIGHFLYERS PUBLICATIONS

ISBN 1-86154-075-2

Published © 1997 by
Booth-Clibborn Editions
12 Percy Street London W1P 9FB

Printed in China

Introductory Text Copyright © 1997 Rob Chapman
Copyright © 1997 Nonconform
Copyright © 1997 Philip Beddard
Copyright © 1997 Booth-Clibborn Editions

ISBN 1-86154-075-2

info@internos.co.uk
www.booth-clibborn-editions.co.uk

Distributed world-wide and by direct mail through
Internos Books, 12 Percy Street,London. W1P 9FB
Distributed in USA by Gingko Press Inc
Distributed in Japan by Tuttle Shokai Inc
Distributed in Hong Kong & Singapore by Page One

ACKNOWLEDGMENTS

Book Design – Nonconform
Project Co-ordinator – Phil Beddard
Project Assistance – Bryan Biggs
Additional Project Assistance – Gavin Brownrigg & Mike Brocken
at Liverpool University Institute of Popular Music's Vinyl Archive
Original Photography – Jonathan Keenan +44 (0)161 236 8283
Additional Photography – Anne Pownall
Introduction – Rob Chapman

Thanks to - Philip Casey . Phil Beddard . Michael Dorrian . Jon Barraclough . Andrew Weatherstone . Mike Carney . John Geary . Stephen A. Wood . Mark Oliver . Gavin Brownrigg . Mike Brocken . Paul Entwistle . Michelle Durkin . Ann Pownall . Jok . Fiona Stroudley (Polydor) . Jez Orakwusi (Sony) . Marion McCormack (EMI) . Melanie Georgiou (Castle Communications) . Steve Ashford (BMG) . Jonathon Bird (Decca) . Gina Spencer (Mercury) . Savina Moman (Carlton) . Frank O'Donnell (Polygram)

Special thanks to - Liz Farrelly . Mark Oliver . Philip Jeck . Bryan Biggs . Gavin Brownrigg . Mike Brocken
The idea for this book was inspired by Live From The Vinyl Junkyard, an exhibition and live art project staged at Bluecoat Gallery Liverpool 1996, curated by Bryan Biggs

Former lyricist and vocalist with Bristol avant punksters The Glaxo Babies, Rob Chapman now makes his living as: cultural historian, broadcaster, conceptualist, music writer, provocateur and all round multi-textualist

INTRODUCTION

BY ROB CHAPMAN

We live in an age of pastiche and plunder. The elevation of kitsch and irony into governing media principles is as evident in sit-coms and kiddies cartoons as it is in advertising and design. The loose configuration of miscellany that gets lumped together under the unsatisfactory catch-all term 'easy listening' is another manifestation of such trends. Many of the records featured in this collection were deeply unfashionable and disposable in their original era but now find themselves 'reclaimed' and enjoying a new lease of life as designers, artists, and audiences alike romp around in the cultural margins and revel in post-modern appreciation. Heritage is well and truly up for grabs.

This has its downside. There may be resonant imagery everywhere but there is cliche and stereotype everywhere too. Discrimination is still valid, even in the midst of high camp and charicature. Kitsch and irony are as capable of becoming hollow conceits as anything else. All too often they represent strategic get out clauses, ways of saying 'oh aren't we being arch and knowing.' The underlying implication is always 'and when we've finished laughing at this stuff we can go back to real art, proper culture'. Once we've parodied all the parodies, and re-appropriated all the appropriations, and the pastiche is all used up, we'll probably start to get all nostalgic about passion and truth to materials again. Rather than view post- modernism as a permanant condition perhaps we should accept it as temporary respite, acknowledge that it's where we go when the old certainties begin to crumble.

But this isn't just about pastiche and plunder and fashionable appropriation, which always has a habit of developing its own rigid orthodoxies no matter how arch and ironic it thinks it's being. Something more significant is occuring too, and these sleeves are testimony to that. Culture is often what goes on when we're looking elsewhere. It's the residue that's left when we've finished scraping off everything that we deem to be significant. Pop music used to fulfill this function admirably. Intellectuals were very slow to come to terms with pop's central paradox: the transient endures. The culturally disenfranchised knew this from the start, of course. As McLuhan pointed out years ago "youth instinctively understands the present environment. It lives mythically and in depth". Less intuitively the cultural elite appropriated rock, and reinvented it in their own image. They burdened it with lit-crit baggage, dressed it in high art hand-me-downs and overloaded it with significance. If we are, as Roland Barthes once said, condemned to speak excessively about reality, then rock music took the full force of that excess. (Message to future civilisations: Some people once thought that rock lyrics could change the world.) Try to imagine a parallel universe in which rock music is an honest indigenous form, no more or less important than Bavarian drinking songs or Polish polka, say, rather than the relentless soundtrack to global imperialism that it has become today. Absorb the images in this book in the same twilight zonal spirit.

If anything we need to rescue the image repertoire of pop culture from a particular set of institutional practices and smart set knowingness and reclaim it for everyone. Truly democratic plunder is as subversive as it gets.

Plate 01 Plate 02 Plate 03

Artist Harry Lubin Symphony Orchestra

Title Music From One Step Beyond

Record Label Decca US

Artist Tom Glazer & Dottie Evans

Title Space Songs

Record Label Motivation Records US

Design Leo Lionni

Artist Peter Appleyard

Title Per-cus-sive Jazz

Record Label RCA UK

Design Irving Sloane

Date 1971

This is where the records in this collection come into their own. Many of them were pitched at that most tenuous of constructions known as 'the mainstream'. Their functionalism and their lack of aspiration is precisely what's made them enduring - the polar opposite of all those rock covers (and rock careers) wrought with significance. The pop process favours casualisation; from promotion to purchase, from the back-room ethos of the session musicians who performed them to the car boot and junk shop nature of their retrieval these products are the authentic ephemera of a throwaway society. To say that they'll be discarded and marginalised again once the fad for pastiche and plunder blows over is to miss the point entirely. Being discarded was always their natural condition. The vinyl junkyard was always their natural habitat.

Now that we live in the age of digitalisation and compact discs, that junkyard can only grow more cluttered and unruly. The new technology may come gift-wrapped in its own ideology, it may have given us pristine sound quality, it may have equalled out all imperfections and delivered clarity in abundance, but at the same time it's has reduced all cover-art to a logo and has shrunk our consumer desires to the size of a bar-code. No doubt in time these clinical criteria will begin to emit their own aura. Sentimentality will once more begin to seep through the cracks and we'll go all dewy eyed remembering proper plastic CD cases. The sleeves in this book evoke a time when our dansette dreams measured 12 by 12 inches and were articulated by a diamond head ploughing through static. Now those dreams measure 5 by 5. They are laser driven and served up in a little plastic tray, like a TV dinner. Maybe it's not just our dreams that got smaller. Although our consumer desires were no less manageable and exploitable then than they are now we fortified ourselves with the knowledge that if we ever missed a mealtime we could get all the nutrients we needed by sucking on a piece of vinyl. Tell that to the kids of today and they'll think you've gone mad.

Record sleeves as we know them, like the recording industry itself, really only came into their own in the aftermath of World War Two. Before 1945 packaging meant plain brown cardboard, the sole function of which was to prevent the brittle old shellac 10-inch 78's, which were usually gathered together in a record album, from grinding into each other. This method of storage is incidentally where the term 'album' for LP's derives from, as do the 1950's sleeve references to tracks being 'in an album' rather than the more contemporary 'on an album'. When 33rpm Long Players were introduced in the late 1940's the standard format was initially the same as the 78 rpm, the 10-inch disc. These were gradually superceded, and surpassed in design value, by the 12 inch disc. Fine art canvases could be as large as a building or as small as a postage stamp. LP sleeves couldn't. Rigid working parameters were therefore imposed right from the start and designers accepted and worked within these confines. The major advantage of LP's, for designers and retailers alike, was that they could be displayed and sifted through in racks, whereas the old 78's were filed side-on like

Plate 04

Plate 05

Plate 06

Artist Bert Kaempfert & His Orchestra
Title Lets Go Bowling
Record Label Polydor UK

Artist Val Merralls Orchestra & Singers
Title Butlins Favourites
Record Label Avenue Recordings UK
Date 1971
Design Brent Gazzaniga

Artist Ruth Wallis
Title How To Stay Sexy Tho' Married
Record Label Mercury UK

books. All the customer could do was peruse the spines, and unlike books there wasn't even the bonus of additional information or illustration on the front cover. The commercial potential of LP design was therefore considerably enhanced with sleeves now serving as advertisements as well as protective packaging. But record sleeves serve another function too. Their emblematic shorthand and their iconography tell us as much about the culture they come from as they do about design values or innovations in technique.

Photography was the most frequently used medium on those early LP sleeves. Indeed the 12-inch record afforded considerable new opportunities for the photographer's art. However these were slow to be realised. Creativity was very much a secondary consideration in the commissioning of sleeve design. The photographer's brief was to 'interpret' the music and this was generally approached in a very literal way. What most clients got was stark portraiture and crass symbolism. The multi-layered possibilities of montage and collage were slow in coming to photographed sleeves. Instead an unwritten hierarchy of suitable materials and appropriate forms soon developed. Abstraction for instance (whether typographical or painterly) was deemed suitable for certain subjects and not others. It is noticeable that on classical music records, (and jazz to some extent) abstraction rather than figurative representation fast became the norm, a design ethos reflecting the music's elevated cultural standing. Indeed those who have previously staked a claim for sleeve design to be validated as

great art have predictably swooped on the classics in order to do so. But prestige and legacy don't stay rooted. They shift historically, culturally, perceptively. The zeitgeist moves on.

High-art aspiration in sleeve design is in fact just as prone to kitsch and obsolescence as the honest products of disposable pop, as a glance at many jazz and classical sleeves from the 1960s and 70s will show you. Abstraction can serve up orthodoxy and linearity like any other design option. By the time many of these sleeves were produced abstraction was already a cliche, a Left Bank anachronism in the age of Pop Art. Clients wanted psuedo Pollock with a smattering of Mondrian and Kandinsky while designers were busy marvelling at the classical form of a coke bottle or a Chevrolet fin.

If the 1950s was the era of innovation in record jacket design it was also a period which saw great advances in (and equally great claims for) recording technology. Hence the appearance here of technical records designed purely for testing your hi-fi hardware. These, along with sound effect records, also favoured abstract design. The future shock of scientific progress could not be contemplated in any figurative sense. It was always more likely to represented by a lithographic squiggle than by a laboratory boffin in a white coat. On the sleeves contained here abstraction was also naturally utilised on anything to do with space (see for instance 'Music from one step beyond' (plate 01) and the Paul Klee pastiche

Plate 07

Plate 08

Plate 09

VJ008

Artist Rusty Warren

Title Rusty Warren Bounces Back
Record Label Jubilee Records US
Design Stephen P. Haapis Studios
Photography Stephen P. Hapis Studios

Artist Woody Woodbury

Title Woody Woodbury's Saloonatics
Record Label Stereoddities US
Date 1961
Photography Sante Schwarm Sheldon

Artist Bert Henry

Title Stag Party Special No.3
Record Label Fax Record Company US
Date 1960

of 'Space Songs.'(plate 02) while the Percussion series, (plate 03) with cover art by Bauhaus teacher Joseph Albers, has been adored and emulated by recent British trip-hop compilations. Equally noteworthy was the sales pitch that advertised technological advances. The scripted rhetoric of progress had a paradoxically archaic beauty all of its own. The blurb on the reverse of Esquivel's 'Exploring new sounds in hi fi' (page 095) reads "This is a New Orthonophonic High Fidelity recording, designed for the phonograph of today or tomorrow. You can buy today without fear of obsolescence in the future." Such sentiments were rendered less effective by the rapidly obsolete and transitory nature of the product.

'Songs for Children' (page 015) depicts a less sophisticated, but no less encompassing engagement with technology. Here the fifties infant, born under the mushroom shadow of the bomb, sits surrounded by brightly coloured discs (children's records were the pioneers of multi coloured vinyl) peering into his dansette dream world.

The tracks on the album are as attuned to the rhythms of time management as any automobile production line. The LP contains tracks specifically designed for 'Fun' 'Learning' and 'Sleep', as well as 'Peas porridge hot' later sampled by De la Soul on their 'De la Soul is dead' LP. For the adults, meanwhile, the cover of Bert Kaempfert's 'Lets go Bowling' (plate 04) with its leisure cameo framed through the competitor's legs, spells Action!, America! Now! Indisputably English is

the Val Merrall Orchestras 'Butlin's Favourites' (plate 05) with its map of Britain indicating Billie Butlin's holiday resorts. Chant them quietly to yourself. Filey. Bognor Regis. Blackpool. A paeon to the three R's of English leisure; regulations, redcoats, and rain. We may have gone ten pin bowling in the UK and enjoyed all the other vicarious imported thrills of Coney Island but we didn't do 'vacation.' We did 'factory fortnight'. The record itself, from the late 1960's, fittingly contains a mixture of military oompah and Tamla covers. Something for the Mums and Dads. Something for the kids. Played for recollection no doubt and then discarded like the memory itself.

Another long gone quirk of the gramophone industry is the LP of music designed to accompany that other great post-war innovation, the home movie. Again you're offered a mood enhancing structure for your leisure dreams. As the liner notes to Eastman Kodaks 'Sound 8' (page 026) put it, "Now, easily and pleasantly, you can add this brightening music to your treasured films - good times with the family, vacations, sports events - together with your own narration, if you wish. And for each show you can choose music to suit your own taste and preference. There's plenty of room for imagination!" On an LP celebrating that other grand American institution 'Barbecue' (page 021) the sleeve note reads "Mothers out in the kitchen, Father's in command, the children are on a holiday at home" and furbish the listener with instructions on appropriate patio furnishings, food and drinks.

Plate 10   Plate 11   Plate 12

Artist Latin All Stars   **Artist** Cardells   **Artist** The Caribbeanas

Title Jazz Heat Bongo Beat   **Title** Limbo Like Me   **Title** Limbo

Record Label Eros UK   **Record Label** Edmar Records Bermuda   **Record Label** Diplomat Records US

Date 1961   **Design** Lee Myles Associates

Design Hobco Arts

Photography 3 Lions Inc

In the age of corporate identity and scientific management these records indicate that every conceivable area of American labour and leisure could be stratified and every layer of stratification had its own sales pitch. Love had the most convoluted language of all. The literal representations of desire etched on these LP covers may be surface impressions but they emanate from a troubled and complex psyche. On 'Music for Lovers Only' (page 126) the terminology is typical of the time; 'Romance', 'Tender Ballads,' 'Relaxed listening moments'. Yet the cover hints at the unspoken intent behind the shorthand of courtship; newly lit cigarettes burn unattended in the ash tray, purse, keys and gloves are discarded beside them, suggesting that the unseen couple couldn't get in the door fast enough before ripping off each other's clothes and collapsing into a frenzy of pent up yearning, suppressed no doubt through endless searching for the correct patio furnishings.

Other polite variants on this theme are equally revealing: 'Music for Holding Hands' (page 126), 'Music for Dreaming (page 146),' with a rather stern looking dreamer, and 'Music for Relaxing (page 137),' with a cover model whose expression suggests she'd like to do more than 'relax'. In contrast to all these hints at carnal shenanigans are 'Music for the Fireside' (page 132) with its air of gendered contentment (pipe and slippers for him, beveridge and chocolates for her) and 101 Strings 'A Bridal Bouquet' (page 130) (an album actually designed to be presented as a wedding gift.) These covers emphasise domestic fulfillment. But such fulfillment soon ebbs into complacency and ennui and other sleeves displayed here hint at sexual neurosis and marital insecurity. There was no shortage of record companies ready to exploit such emotions. Albums like 'How to stay sexy tho' married' (plate 06) by Ruth 'innuendo dispenser' Wallis, and the 'sinsational' Rusty Warren's 'Bounces Back' (plate 07), were promoted on the premise that flagging marriages could be made more bearable with the help of a little hi-fi pick me up. Men got their light relief from 'saucy' adult humour records which were often only available from Mail Order Record Clubs. Those included here range from the impish but never too vulgar 'Saloonantics' (plate 08) by Woody Woodbury to the more risque wisecracks of Adam magazine's 'Stag Party Special' (plate 09) albums (whose back covers advertised a 'speciality series' of Erotica LP's with titles like 'Passion, Pain and Pleasure'.) These adult swinger albums sold in their thousands without ever appearing on any pop chart. Today, though, they have all but disappeared. The territory has been conceded to under the counter hardcore at one extreme and seaside postcard titillation at the other.

The sexuality subtext took many forms, and remains perenially ripe for appropriation. Behind every encoded hetero assumption etched on these sleeves there was an abundance of closeted iconography struggling to break free. The girl on the cover of Surprise Records 'For Adults Only' (page 102) could have passed as, in fact might have been, a rather gorgeous drag queen. The cover of UTC's 'Ladies of Burlesque' (page 103) on the other hand depicts a forlorn looking Rae/Ray Bourbon ("world's foremost female

Plate 13

Plate 14

VJ010

Artist Various

Title It's Trad Dad

Record Label Columbia/EMI UK

Date 1962

Artist Various

Title Teenage A Go-Go

Record Label Columbia Canada

impersonator"). Her expression seems to say, 'Look my name is in lights but my life is somehow tragic'. The mere availability of such albums speaks volumes about the repressed voyeuristic desires that lay behind the period's all-American ideals.

Nowhere was this better illustrated than in the depictions of exoticism that graced many a 1950's LP. The covers to 'Mambo's and chachacha's,' 'Jazz Heat Bongo Beat,' (plate 10) and 'Limbo like me' (plate 11) exploit a common racial motif. An impassioned caucasian female dancer responds to the tom-tom rythms of a hidden black man. Only his hands are visible. The dancing is not overtly suggestive but the sub-text smoulders with possibilities. When the participants are depicted in more visibly suggestive guises, as on The Caribbeana's' 'Limbo,' (plate 12) or Sunny Burke and his Orchestra's 'Lets Mambo' (page 156), the whole scene is conveniently shrouded in silhouette. English versions of exotica tended to be milder and more literal, usually settling for a set of bongo drums, an inane (rather than possessed) dancer and a tiger skin rug - although in the case of the Hunter's 'Teen Scene' (page 047) the colonial spoils appear to have been brought back to a field in Hertfordshire! Windmill's 'Pop Explosion Sitar Style' (page 104) from Sagram with its mock 'eastern' typographics is Sixties kitsch exotica par excellence. The mustachioed hippie brute in bathrobe surrounded by adoring girls and hookah was the secret fantasy of every ageing flower child made flesh. The fact that he doesn't look like he's been further east than Dagenham only adds to the kitsch value. Generally, though, the primal

undertow of UK exotica was more tellingly evoked in sleeve notes than cover imagery. Take 'Latin Hits I Missed' (page 177) by Edmundo Ros and his Orchestra for example, where the liner notes read: "the sultry beckoning saxophone, the compelling throb of the bongos, the wood flute's primeval lure, the mysterious hush of muted trumpets and horns, the surging warmth of violins....deep in the jungle the syncopated pulse beat of drums entice you closer to the undergrowth."

Other sleeves reveal a more simple psychology, ie popular culture's relentless pursuit of the profit motive. Cash-ins and crazes characterise this collection. Power Pak's compilation 'The Streak' (page 150) was hastily released to exploit what was expected to be a short lived American dormitory trend of running butt naked through public places. The cover acknowledges this by showing nothing but the bottom half of an athletic leg, a fleeting glimpse and it's gone. The record is if anything even more faithful to this ethos. It contains the novelty hit 'The streak' and eight totally unrelated fillers such as 'Harper Valley PTA' and 'Seasons in the Sun'.

Dancing is naturally a favoured motif on many of these records. On 'It's Trad Dad' (plate 13) (from the Columbia motion picture) the cover replicates a concert or cinema poster. Here the billing dwarfs the gyrating human figures even though the film itself was a celebration of teenage exuberance. LP's from the height of the swinging 60's such as

Plate 15

Plate 16

Artist Alan Moorhouse Orchestra

Title Beatles Bach & Bacharach Go Bossa

Record Label MFP/EMI UK

Date 1971

Design Clare Osborn

Photography Brian Tyer

Artist Various

Title Le Bon Vieux Temps Du Twist

Record Label MFP/EMI France

Photography Laguens

'Teenage a go go,' (plate 14) with its gyrating girl in a cage, present stock images of unleashed desire. On a lot of the 1960's and 70's covers though couples strike awkward poses with little of the style and grace of previous dance eras. This is in itself shrewdly referential, mirroring the gradual downgrading of finesse that occured as strict tempo and formation dancing gave way to unbridled freestyle. For the rythmically challenged there was a considerable price to pay. The helplessly swaying dude caught in a tragedy of posture on the cover of 'Beatles Bach Bacharach go Bossa' (plate 15) suggests we'd come a long way from the forbidden limbos of the fifties, but in many ways we were no more liberated. By the 1970s such covers were populated by, and aimed at, suburban would-be swingers, even though there is possibly nothing more startling than the English would-be swinger 'letting his hair down'. It is this chasm between the intent and the actual that makes this type of cover look so deliciously inappropriate now. On the LP by easy-listening king Klaus Wunderlich the title screams 'We got rhythm' (page 082) while the pose of the dancers suggests otherwise. Other examples are just plain demented. On 'Twist!' (plate 16) featuring Dick Rivers, Burt Blanca, and Richard Anthony a man in MacArthur Park style 'stripped pair of pants' threatens to decapitate his dolly bird companions as he leaps through the air. This may be a reference to the legend of 'Perkins from Accounts,' who, drunk on Mateus Rose and lack of inhibition, actually killed a girl on a Scarborough ballroom floor. Believed to be the only known case of death by reckless dancing, it became a popular urban myth of the 1960s.

The uneasy collision between squareness and hip doesn't just manifest itself in the cover art. The graphics scream their own confusion of emphasis and lack of clarity. Take 'example X' (plate 17) where the billing reads from the top down; 'Crystal Blue Pursuasion' (one song on the album) 'Sounds of Today' (hack generic youth-speak for the type of song) 'Orange Groove' (the backing singers we assume at first glance) and 'The sounds of the new generation' (the artists? maybe another genre type? We aren't sure.) This indiscriminate bombardment of information flattens everything to one dimensional surface and uniform emphasis. The perfect post modern metaphor. Elsewhere song titles spill out in a riot of mismatched typography which subverts all our rockist notions of a star system. The abundance of cover version LPs that were released in the 1960s and early 1970s challenge rock music's market ideologies by their very existence. At their peak the albums released on such labels as Music for Pleasure and Marble Arch were disqualified from the sales charts. The horror of an LP Top 10 flooded with the budget price residue of a bargain bin popular culture was too much for the record industry to contemplate. It had its hierarchies to uphold. Rock fetishises significance, authenticity and integrity, but the subversive mainstream just wanted the familiarity of a good tune and a regular knees up. Take the evident priorities of Boulevard Record's 'Party Fever' (plate 18). Its cover foregrounds the 'hits of the day' contained on the record and centres on a party raver whose gaze is suspiciously ecstatic, but there in the background are Mum and Dad, maybe even Gran and Grandad, keeping a watchful benevolent eye on pop culture. At other times there's something

Plate 17

Plate 18

VJ012

Artist The Orange Groove

Title Crystal Blue Persuasion & Other
Sounds Of Today

Record Label Somerset US

Artist Various

Title Party Fever

Record Label Boulevard Records UK

Date 1974

savagely profound in the crude and literal reductionism on display. What
more sardonic critique of teeny hysteria is there than The Metro Records' LP
'Herman's Hermits Greatest Hits played by the Liverpool Strings' (page 199)
which reduces Herman, maybe the entire Merseybeat boom, to a moptop
wig plonked unceremoniously onto a guitar head.

If the agenda for the 1960s was determined by the media establishment of
swinging London the 1970s was far more sexually subversive. Provincial
permissiveness was up for grabs. Everyone could live out their own low rent
Karma Sutra. Designers reflected this in their erratic handling of eroticism.
On the cover of Zack Lawrence's *'Alive 'An'Kickin' (plate 19)* album a troupe
of girls do the high kicking splits in mini skirts, exposing the pudenda zone in
the most casually unerotic way imaginable. The Music For Pleasure Hot Hits
series was an equally rich source of gauche and ungainly sexploitation. The
phallocentric imagery of the bow and arrow girl on *'Hot Hits 11' (plate 20)*
might have had more credence if they could have been bothered to line it up
properly. But it is precisely here, in the not quite getting it right, where the
retrospective appeal lies. This is why the more traditional porno fare of
gaping and glossy open mouths that adorn some of these covers now look so
hackneyed and 'rock and roll' in comparison. We've used up that particular
literal language of desire. It's too tied up with a discredited hetero male gaze.

What these covers do is capture each eras notion of idealised female
sexuality. In the 1950s Lollabrigida lookalikes predominate, all hips and high-
tech brassieres. They gave way to the stoned inanimate waifs of the diet pill
pushing sixties. Dolly birds casually draped about art deco furnishings or in
dreamy absent reverie by the record player may speak to us through the
fixtures and fittings of earlier eras but they do so via a lexicon of impeccably
Sixties postures. In time, of course, even the casually submissive pose of the
girl on the cover of The Duncan Lamont Orchestra's *'This Guy' (page 150)* will
look as though it has been handed down from antiquity. Seventies cover
nudes were more brazen, defiant, and hyper real. Witness the mutilating
reflection of the woman on the cover of *'Love on Love' (page 142)*. She looks
as though she's melting, doll-like. She might even represent an inflatable -
the album itself appears to have been designed as a sex aid. Sixties images
of nakedness seem far more staid and decorative in comparison. Models
adorned in body paint were initially favoured to convey the psychedelic life
but like mini skirts, acid flashbacks, and unfit-for-habitation tower blocks,
they lingered on into the seventies indiscriminantly adorning anything from
continental interpretations of UK hits to cover versions of tracks made
famous by Tom Jones. But by then it was too late to turn back. We couldn't
unlearn the sign language of pop. Everything outlives its sell-by date.
Especially the things we think most likely to perish.

Loungecore Update. Spring Equinox 2525. Future civilisations will continue
to chance upon these artifacts and, depending on the prevailing cultural
climate and the vagaries of fashion, they will either worship or revile them.
Recent fundamentalist attempts to discredit DNA and the carbon dating
wars of the early 24th century are having as profound an effect as the

Plate 19

Plate 20

Artist The Zack Laurence Orchestra

Title Alive An' Kickin

Record Label DJM Records UK

Date 1969

Design Jim Goff

Artist Various

Title Hot Hits II

Record Label MFP/EMI UK

Date 1972

Design Terry Beard

Photography Jack Wood & Terry Beard

evolutionist versus creationist theories of earlier times, and it is expected that future explorers will be anything up to 1,000 years out in their estimates of where these beautiful laminated cardboard objects came from. Those who had grown nostalgic for the post-modernist cults of the late 20th century found it ironic indeed that science and history should still be engaged in such quaint combat. Others celebrated, believing that mythology is the lifeblood of popular culture. They petitioned for a law to be passed restricting the amount of daylight that could be cast on magic. Hardline anarcho-sensualists continued to insist that only magic can be multi-layered onto magic and that meaning should always be up for grabs. Their most recent communique read as follows: "These record covers are our little Turin shrouds, our pagan pleasures, our wrapped plastic totems, our patented other world, our phantasy forum, our forget me nots, our cake out in the rain, and we'll never have that recipe again." Experts are still baffled by that last line. They think it might be some kind of code.

Rob Chapman.

"Try not to use a needle pressure that will damage the record. A damaged record is an unhappy record" Anon

Artist *Kiddieland Chorus*
Title *Songs For Children*
Record Label *Somerset Records USA*

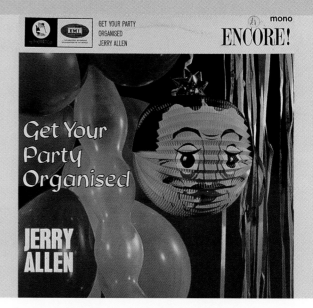

"What makes a party a success? It helps if the party giver has the knack of making sure the drinks never run out, that the males don't outnumber the females, and that whatever is on the record player will make the party swing like a bomb or purr like a sports car in top gear." **Anon**

Artist Victor Silvester & Orchestra	**Artist** Jerry Allen
Title Lets Have A Dancing Party	**Title** Get Your Party Organised
Record Label EMI UK	**Record Label** Encore/EMI UK
Date 1959	**Date** 1965
Photography Picturepoint Ltd	

Artist Mrs Mills

Title It's Party Time

Record Label EMI UK

Date 1964

Photography Houston Rogers

Artist Mrs Mills

Title Everybody's Welcome At
Mrs Mills Party

Record Label EMI UK

Date 1963

Artist Mrs Mills

Title Mrs Mills Party

Record Label EMI UK

Date 1965

Artist Sydney Thompson

Title Party Dances

Record Label Sydney Thompson Records UK

Photography Jack Blake

"Any time is the time to celebrate. It could be a wedding, an anniversary, a homecoming . . . so many reasons can call for celebration or maybe no reason at all. Just the mere joy of living could make every day a time to celebrate." **Anon**

Artist *Russ Conway*

Title *Time To Celebrate*

Record Label *Columbia/EMI UK*

Date *1959*

Photography *Angus McBean*

Artist *Russ Conway*

Title *Party Time*

Record Label *Columbia/EMI UK*

Date *1960*

"Here is an opportunity to present your own personal request programme - no need to go on hoping that the luck of the draw will come your way, for here is a selection of well loved melodies which have not out-stayed their welcome. It is because the songs themselves have an unpretentious charm that they have been cherished through the years. They strike a responsive chord the minute they are heard, recapturing romantic moments moments, happy family gatherings or pleasurable jaunts." **Anon**

Artist Russ Conway	**Artist** Ken Griffin	**Artist** The White Sisters
Title Family Favourites	**Title** Lets Have A Party (And Everybody Sing)	**Title** Bless This House
Record Label Columbia/EMI UK	**Record Label** Phillips UK	**Record Label** Word UK
Date 1959	**Date** 1958	**Date** 1955
Photography Flair		

Artist Various

Title The World Of Your Hundred Best Tunes Vol 3

Record Label Decca UK

Date 1972

Photography David Wedgbury

Artist Various

Title The World Of Your Hundred Best Tunes Vol 6

Record Label Decca UK

Date 1973

Photography Suzette Stephens

Artist Various

Title The World Of Your Hundred Best Tunes Vol 9

Record Label Decca UK

Date 1975

Artist Various

Title The World Of Your Hundred Best Tunes Vol 10

Record Label Decca UK

Date 1975

Photography John Thompson

"Soft music, cool drinks, a shady corner - what could be more gracious and pleasant on a hot afternoon! And in the evening, what better living than a barbecue in your own backyard, or on your patio, porch or terrace, surrounded by family and friends, and by music especially selected for your out-door living! Mothers out of tthe kitchen, father's in command, the children are on a holiday at home, the meat is cooking and the corn is roasting." **Anon**

Artist Peter Barclay & His Orchestra

Title Barbeque

Record Label Columbia US

Photography Hedrich Blessing

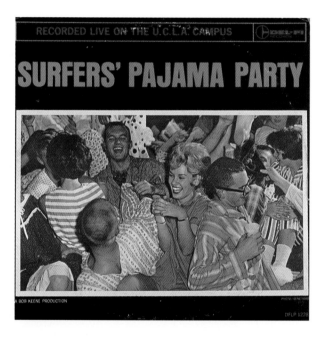

VJ022

Artist Sandy Nelson

Title Teenage House Party

Record Label Imperial US

Date 1963

Artist The Centurians

Title Surfers Pyjama Party

Record Label Del-Fi US

Photography Gene Ford

"Imagine the glistening sheen of 58 strings, the bright song of woodwinds, the full-throated roar of a large brass section. Add the jungle throb of drums, the Latin flavour of mandolins and guitars, and the exotic colour of bongos and timbales. Now you're ready for a fascinating tonal trip around the world." **Herman Kaplan**

Artist The International Pop Orchestra
Title An Exciting Evening At Home With The
International Pop Orchestra
Record Label Cameo US
Date 1962
Design Al Cahn & Miller, Bodden & Rich Inc

Artist Arne Oit
Title Estonian Hits
Record Label Meloodia USSR
Date 1975

Artist Klaus Wunderlich
Title Sound Moog 2000, Organ Rhythm
Record Label Telefunken/Decca Germany
Date 1973

RECORD 1
YOU DO SOMETHING TO ME
THEY CAN'T TAKE THAT AWAY FROM ME
HELLO, YOUNG LOVERS
WHERE OR WHEN
ALL THE THINGS YOU ARE
PEOPLE WILL SAY WE'RE IN LOVE

ON THE STREET WHERE YOU LIVE
MOONLIGHT SERENADE
THE WAY YOU LOOK TONIGHT
AS TIME GOES BY
SMOKE GETS IN YOUR EYES
LULLABY OF BIRDLAND

RECORD 2
CHEEK TO CHEEK
THANKS FOR THE MEMORY
EASY TO LOVE
LAURA
IT MIGHT AS WELL BE SPRING
WARSAW CONCERTO

I COULD HAVE DANCED ALL NIGHT
I'VE GROWN ACCUSTOMED TO HER FACE
AN IMPROVISATION ON 'LIEBESTRAUM'
YOUNG AT HEART
AN IMPROVISATION ON
'DANCE OF THE SUGAR PLUM FAIRY'
I'LL SEE YOU AGAIN

"The frequency range of this recording encompasses the abysmal 3 cps as well as the astronomical 39,582 cps! and although these extremes cannot be detected by the ordinary human ear, they can be heard by very small children and people suffering from certain rare forms of dementia praecox. It is our opinion, however, that if these lower and upper frequences were omitted, a certain warmth of tone that is sensed and felt, rather than merely heard, would be lost forever to those between the ages of 2 and 107 who have healthy dementias and praecoxes." **Anon**

Artist Various

Title The Enjoyment Of Music

Record Label EMI UK

Date 1968

Photography Anthony Lloyd-Parker

Artist Ray Conniff Orchestra

Title Hi Fi Companion

Record Label CBS UK

Design Verity Graphic Arts

Photography David Lowe

Artist Jack Marshall
Title Soundsville
Record Label Capitol US
Date 1959

"These beautifully recorded musical selections are adaptable to just about every situation you are likely to capture on film. Now easily and pleasantly, you can add this brightening music to your treasured films - good times with the family, vacations, sports events - together with your own narration, if you wish. And for each show, you can choose music to suit your own taste and preference . . . there's plenty of room for imagination!" **Anon**

Artist Original Sound Recording

Title Sound 8 Background Music Vol 1

Record Label Eastman Kodac US

Artist Norman Paris

Title The Perfect Background Music For Your Home Movies

Record Label MGM US

Date 1964

Photography Burt Owen

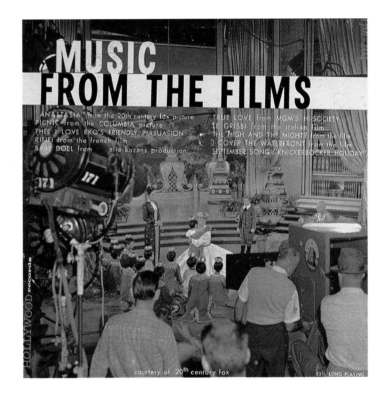

Artist Steve Race & His Orchestra

Title Dance To The T.V. Themes

Record Label World Record Club Ltd UK

Date 1969

Photography Karil Evans

Artist Various

Title Music From The Films

Record Label Hollywood US

Date 1957

Artist Mantovani & His Orchestra

Title Mantovani Film Encores

Record Label Decca UK

Date 1958

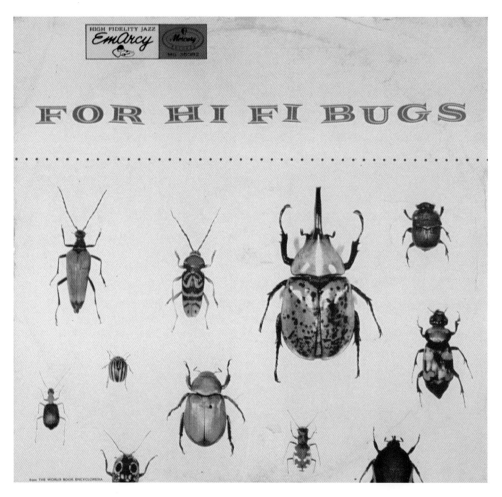

"Music is so intensely personal, so much a matter of what you yourself feel - and let the rules go hang - that the only sensible basis on which you should build your library is personal choise. If you like it, then by all means it belongs in your record collection. Enjoy it and play with pride." **Anon**

Artist Pete Rugolo Orchestra
Title For Hi Fi Bugs
Record Label Mercury UK
Date 1956

"Listening to music which is well performed is a fine experience for children, especially when the record player equipment is good, as it should always be. But there is more to music than listening. There is also living it. When a kid has a big person who can make up songs with him and just for him, with perhaps his own name in the verses, plus things he knows personally, like doorbells, dogs, fire engines and bird houses, then he is living music." **Lee Hays**

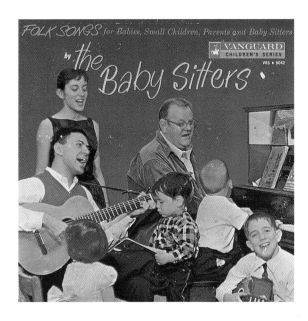
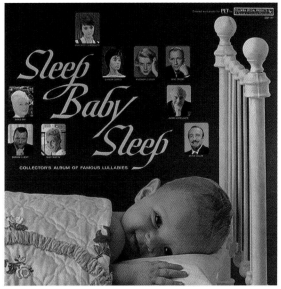

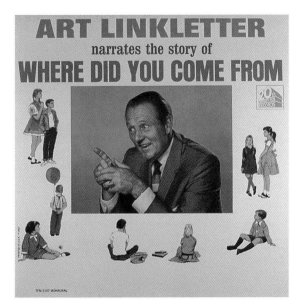

Artist The Baby Sitters

Title Folk Songs For Babies, Small Children, Parents & Baby Sitters

Record Label Vanguard US

Artist Various

Title Sleep Baby Sleep

Record Label Columbia US

Date 1958

Artist Art Linkletter

Title Where Did You Come From

Record Label 20th Century Fox US

Date 1963

Design Moskof Morrison Inc

Artist Steve Allen

Title How To Think

Record Label Gifted Childrens Monthly US

Date 1965

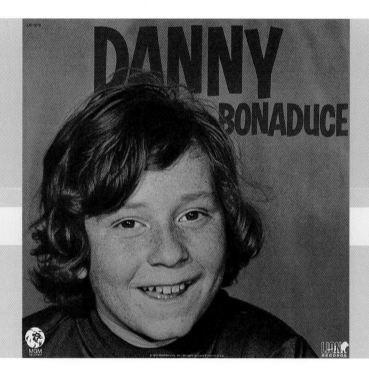

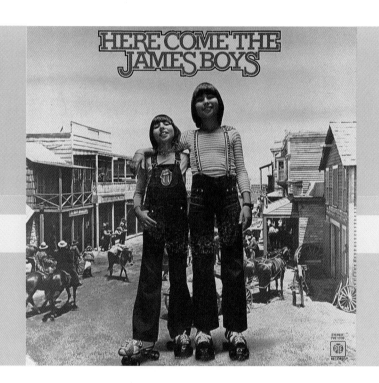

Artist Danny Bonaduce

Title Danny Bonaduce

Record Label MGM/Lion Records US

Date 1972

Artist The James Boys

Title Here Come The James Boys

Record Label Pye US

Date 1973

Design DFK/David Krieger

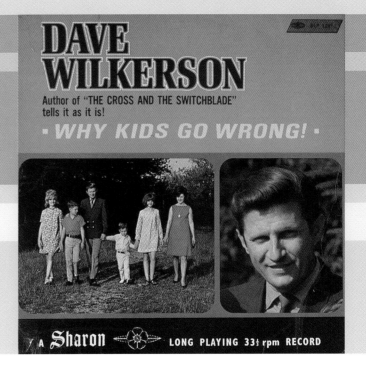

Artist The Groovy Gang
Title Songs For Swinging Children
Record Label Contour

Artist Dave Wilkerson
Title Why Kids Go Wrong
Record Label Zondervan US
Date 1952

Artist Scotty Alexander
Title Here I Come World
Record Label Vector Records US
Date 1980
Design Scott Sakamoto
Photography John Emmerling

Artist *Ray Conniff & His Orchestra*

Title *'s Wonderful 's Marvellous*

Record Label *CBS UK*

Date *1957*

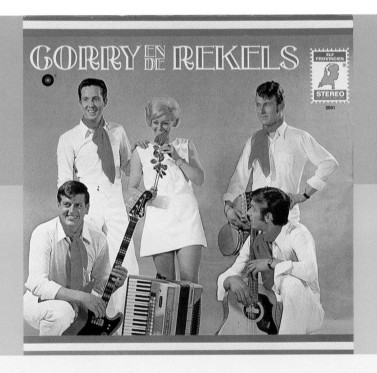

Artist Corry En De Rekels

Record Label Dureco Holland

Date 1969

Artist Corry En De Rekels

Record Label Dureco Holland

Date 1969

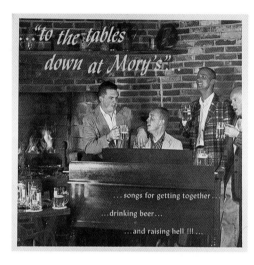

"There are countless songs for listening, dancing, and for everything from film backgrounds to nerve-racking radio commercials, but the best loved songs are those that everyone can sing. These are simple, familiar tunes that give all of us a lift. The singing of them are the best remembered moments of any get-together." **Anon**

Artist Various

Title Prosit - German Beer Drinking Songs

Record Label EMI UK

Date 1963

Photography Aetlier Robert Pütz

Artist Lee Gotch's Ivy Barflies

Title To The Tables Down At Mory's

Record Label Miller US

Date 1957

Artist Eileen Donaghy with Chorus & Orchestra

Title Sing The Old Favourites

Record Label Fontana UK

Date 1961

Artist *The Jay Norman Quintet*

Title *The Cocktail Hour*

Record Label *ARC UK*

Date *1963*

Photography *W.E. Kimp*

Artist *Various*

Title *Hammond Dancing Ohne Pause*

Record Label *Decca Germany*

Photography *Kleinhempel*

Artist J.D & Dallas

Title Keep It Country

Record Label Klub Records Ltd US

Date 1981

Photography Gavin McNae

Artist Various

Title That Dobro Sound Goin' Round

Record Label Starday/Gusto US

Date 1954

Photography Terry Tomlin

Artist Homer & Jethro

Title Homer & Jethro At The Country Club

Record Label RCA US

Date 1960

Artist Herman & Angie

Title Sing Me Back Home

Record Label Emerald/Decca UK

Date 1978

Artist Del & Sue Smart

Title Singing Country Favorites

Record Label Somerset US

Artist The Kendalls

Title Heavens Just A Sin Away

Record Label Ovation US

Date 1976

Design Herb Bruce/Bob Dorobiala

Artist Betty & Joe Springer

Title Songs By Betty & Joe Springer Of HCJB

Record Label Diaden Productions Inc US

Artist Al Lerner

Title A Tribute To Eddie Duchin

Record Label Tops US

"Theres no question in my mind, you'll enjoy this album. You'll tell your friends about it, you'll treasure it, you'll thank-goodness for it. Only for the sake of your family name and honor, your civic pride and stature - ask the clerk to wrap it in brown paper. Go ahead be weak for a minute - buy the damn album! After all who knows? maybe crazy josé is your mother! **Ed Sherman**

Artist Crazy José
Title Cha Cha Cha
Record Label United Artists US
Date 1959
Design Lean Bacon
Photography Harris Divine

"They are a group that uses soul and mind and heart to make music. They are not fake or phoney, theirs is a music and a sound which pleases and touches and communicates whether it be a song as free and happy as the wind on a summer day or a song which reveals a darker vision of life. **Peter Reilly**

Artist The Gordian Knot

Title The Gordian Knot

Record Label Verve/MGM US

Design Dick Smith

Photography Don Ornitz

Artist Joe Jr & The Side Effects

Title Tribute

Record Label Diamond Hong Kong

Date 1967

Photography James Fong

Artist Joe Jr

Title Exclusively Yours By Joe Jr

Record Label Diamond Hong Kong

Date 1968

Photography Edward Gamarekian

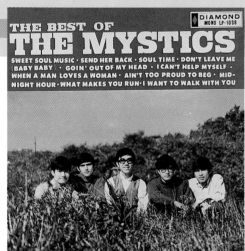

Artist *The Lettermen*

Title *First Class*

Record Label *Stag Music UK*

Date *1973*

Design *Cornelius*

Artist *The New Vaudeville Band*

Title *Winchester Cathedral*

Record Label *Fontana UK*

Date *1966*

Artist *The Blue Magnolia Jass Orchestra*

Title *Yes, Sir, It's Blue Magnolia Jass Orchestra*

Record Label *SRT Productions UK*

Photography *Arthur Waite*

Artist *The Mystics*

Title *The Best Of The Mystics*

Record Label *Diamond Hong Kong*

Date *1968*

"It is the kind of sound that makes you sit up and take notice for sheer professionalism and dedication - nothing sloppy about this outfit. Tempo interpretation, mood, precision, it is all here." **Anon**

Artist Harmony Revival	**Artist** The Miami Show Band	**Artist** The Ken Thompson Sound	**Artist** Big Tom & The Travellers	**Artist** Frank Jennings Syndicate
Title Harmony Revival	**Title** The Miami All Stars	**Title** Just For You	**Title** When The Roses Bloom Again	**Title** Ponderosa Country
Record Label Swan Records UK	**Record Label** PYE UK	**Record Label** Fairworld UK	**Record Label** Denver Records UK	**Record Label** One Up/EMI UK
Date 1974	**Date** 1967		**Date** 1975	

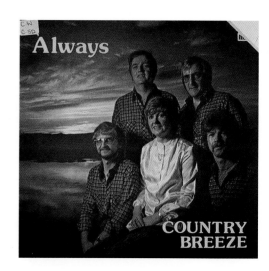

Artist Charley Boy	**Artist** The Orange Blossom Sound	**Artist** Country Breeze
Title Introducing Charley Boy	**Title** The Exciting Orange Blossom Sound	**Title** Always
Record Label Release Records Ltd Ireland	**Record Label** Hallmark/Pickwick UK	**Record Label** Klub Records Ltd UK
Design Diana O'Donnell	**Date** 1969	**Date** 1981
Photography Graham Spencer		**Photography** Brian Sherman

Artist Asleep At The Wheel

Title Comin' Right At Ya

Record Label Sunset Records UK

Design Lloyd Ziff/Mike Salisbury

Photography Jim Marshall

Artist The Sheba Sound

Title The Sheba Sound

Record Label BBC UK

Date 1977

Design Mario Moscardini/Paul Chave

Photography Dupes Associates

"Showbusiness history abounds with instances of clever gimmicks that bring instant but fleeting success. The real talents are those who, having somehow hit the top manage to stay there and become a permanent part of their particular sphere." **Anon**

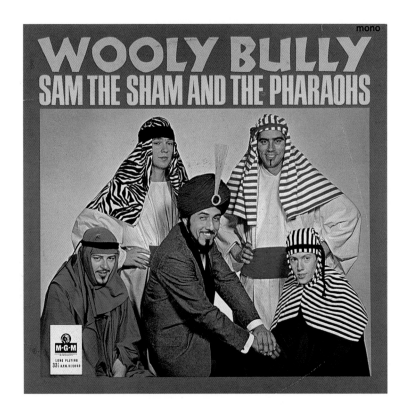

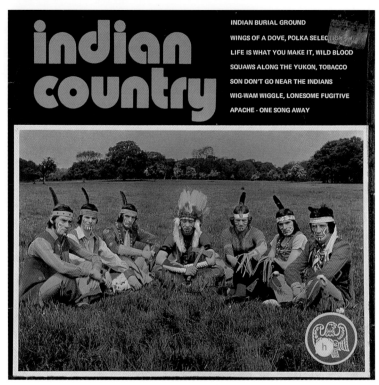

Artist Sam The Sham & The Pharaohs

Title Wooly Bully

Record Label EMI UK

Date 1965

Photography Bill & Joy Webb

Artist The Indians

Title Indian Country

Record Label Hawk Records Ireland

Date 1972

Design Paddy Burns

Artist Los Indios Tabajaras

Title The Best Of Los Indios Tabajaras

Record Label RCA UK

Date 1970

Artist The Hunters
Title Teen Scene
Record Label Fontana UK
Date 1963

Artist Eartha Kit
Title Down To Eartha
Record Label RCA/Victor UK
Date 1955
Photography David B. Hecht

Artist Bert Kaempfert & His Orchestra
Title A Swingin' Safari
Record Label Polydor UK
Date 1962

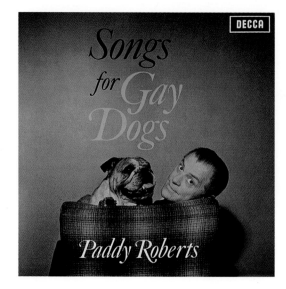

Artist Kenn Dodd

Title Hits For Now & Always

Record Label Columbia/EMI UK

Date 1962

Artist Don Elliott & His Choir

Title The Mello Sound

Record Label Brunswick/Decca UK

Date 1954

Photography Ylla from Rapho Guillumette

Artist Paddy Roberts

Title Songs For Gay Dogs

Record Label Decca UK

Date 1963

"Take dogs for example. We may have guard dogs, gundogs, sheep dogs, guide dogs, race dogs, space dogs. Cats may attract us by their grace and beauty or repel us by their apparent untamed savagery. We may be for dogs and against cats. We may recoil from the canine overture and welcome the feline advance. Whatever our feelings maybe, it is hoped that this record will at least bring pleasure to some of Britains animal lovers." **Anon**

 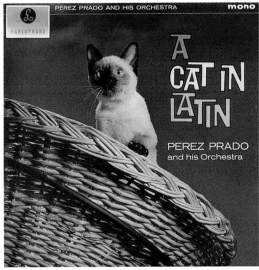 

Artist Stanley Black

Title Sophisticat In Cuba

Record Label Decca UK

Date 1958

Photography Hans Wild

Artist Perez Prado & His Orchestra

Title A Cat In Latin

Record Label EMI UK

Date 1964

Artist The Jay Norman Quintet

Title Somebody Loves Me

Record Label Society/ARC UK

Date 1963

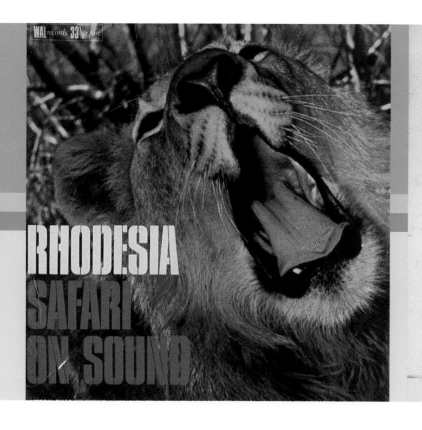

Cats and Dogs

RED 54M

the history of cats and dogs, with recordings of domestic and wild
species by Ludwig Koch, Eric Simms, John Burton and Roger Perry

BBC Wildlife Series No. 3

Artist Various	**Artist** Original Sound Recordings
Title Rhodesia Safari On Sound	**Title** Cats & Dogs
Record Label Wal Records Rhodesia	**Record Label** BBC UK
Design Neil Pederson	**Date** 1967
Photography Big Game Photography (PVT) Ltd	**Photography** Sally Anne Thompson

THE PETERSON FIELD GUIDE TO THE
SR BIRD SONGS
RECORDS OF BRITAIN AND EUROPE

ELECTRONIC
STEREO

Record 8

HMA 246

BIRD SOUNDS IN CLOSE-UP
RECORDED & COMPILED BY
VICTOR C. LEWIS

HALLMARK
MONO

VJ**051**

Artist Sture Palmer & Jeffery Boswall
Title Bird Songs Of Britain & Europe
Record Label Sweden Records
Date 1972
Design Lasse H. Halldin

Artist Original Sound Recordings
Title Bird Sounds In Close Up
Record Label Hallmark/Pickwick UK
Date 1969

Artist Alan Povey

Title Owd Grandad Piggot

Record Label Midland Sound Recordings UK

Date 1977

Photography Dave Hastilow

Artist Lord Birkett

Title The Art Of Advocacy

Record Label Decca UK

Date 1962

Artist Joe E. Ross

Title Love Songs From A Cop

Record Label Columbia/EMI UK

Date 1964

Artist Bill Doggett

Title "Hold It"

Record Label Gusto US

Date 1975

Artist Brian Maxine
Title King Of The Ring
Record Label Starline/EMI UK
Date 1972

Artist Allan Smethurst
Title The Best Of The Singing Postman
Record Label Starline/EMI UK
Date 1966

Artist Various
Title Introduction To Jazz by
The Rev A.L. Kershaw
Record Label Brunswick/Decca UK
Date 1956

Artist The Coney Island Harmoneers
Title Barber Shop Quartet Favourites
Record Label Hollywood US

Artist Tex Williams

Title Smoke Smoke Smoke

Record Label Stetson/Capitol US

Date 1960

Artist Various

Title Skeets McDonalds Tattooed Lady

Record Label Fortune Records US

Date 1961

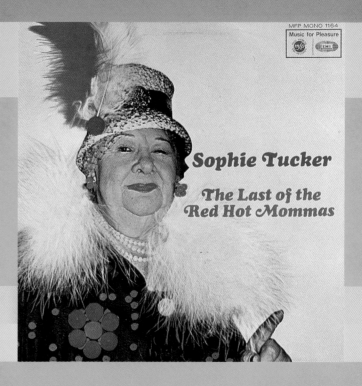

Artist Philomena Begley

Title Truckin' Queen

Record Label Ritz Records UK

Date 1977

Photography David Dugal

Artist Sophie Tucker With Ted Shapiro & Orchestra

Title The Last Of The Red Hot Mommas

Record Label MFP/EMI UK

Date 1968

Design Haydon Young

Photography Keystone

Artist Johnny Handle

Title She's A Big Lass She's A Bonny Lass

Record Label One Up/EMI UK

Date 1978

Design Feref

Photography Rayment Kirby

Artist Hamish Imlach

Title The Two Sides Of Hamish Imlach

Record Label Transatlantic Records UK

Date 1968

Design Brian Shuel

INTRODUCING

BIG GEORGE

INSTITUTE OF POPULAR MUSIC

BLANKET ON THE GROUND
HAPPY TO BE ON AN
ISLAND IN THE SUN
THE LAST FAREWELL
DON'T STAY AWAY TOO LONG
FOR THE GOOD TIMES
DOWN IN THE GLEN
& OTHERS

emerald gem

"Talent comes in a variety of packages - short, tall, fat, thin, short hair, long hair, red, yellow, black or white, you name it talent fits any package." **Anon**

Artist Big George
Title Introducing Big George
Record Label Emerald Gem/Decca UK
Date 1977

Artist Juicy Lucy

Title Juicy Lucy

Record Label Vertigo UK

Date 1969

Design Nigel Thomas, Glen Campbell & Peter Smith

Photography Peter Smith

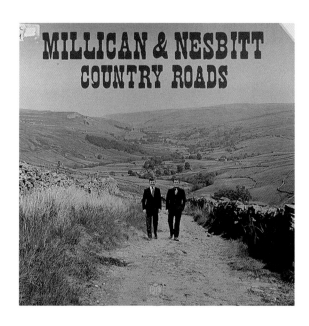

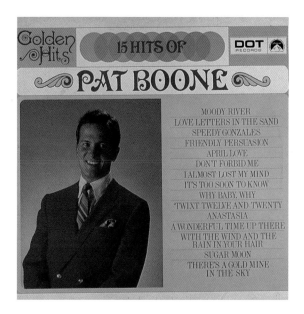

Artist Sam Levenson

Title But Seriously Folks

Record Label Hanover/Signature US

Date 1955

Artist Alistair Cooke

Title An Evening With Alistair Cooke

Record Label CBS UK

Date 1955

Design Roslav Szaybo & M. Boncza

Photography Brian Griffin

Artist Millican & Nesbitt

Title Country Roads

Record Label PYE UK

Date 1978

Design Design Machine

Artist Pat Boone

Title Golden Hits

Record Label EMI UK

Date 1963

Design Studio Five Inc

Photography Studio Five Inc

"Heck everyone knows the story of the poor farm boy out of Drumakill, Ireland, who got a few friends together around Castleblayney one day, formed a band and started 'Pickin and Grinnin' for the folks. How they struggled along for pennies, until that lucky night they appeared on T.V. to fill a few 'extra minutes' of time. How on this lucky night, music history was made." **Tex Farr**

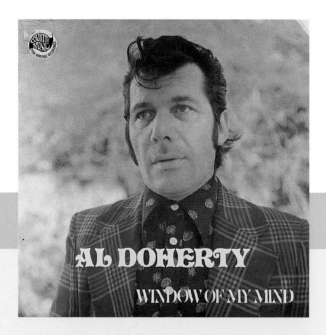

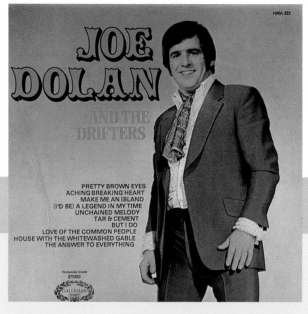

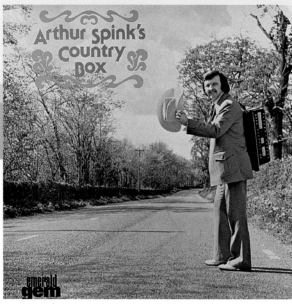

Artist Al Doherty

Title Window Of My Mind

Record Label Folk Heritage Wales

Date 1975

Design Norman C. Lees

Photography Alan Green

Artist Joe Dolan

Title Joe Dolan & The Drifters

Record Label Hallmark/Pickwick UK

Artist Arthur Spink

Title Arthur Spink's Country Box

Record Label Decca UK

Date 1979

Photography Ziggy Nowak-Solinski

Artist Big Tom & The Mainliners

Title Souvenirs

Record Label Denver Records UK

Date 1975

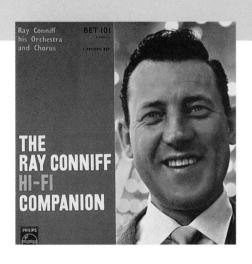

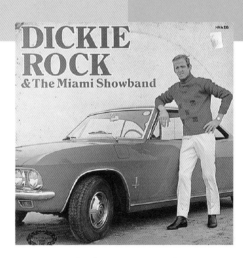

Artist Ray Merrell

Title Only You

Record Label Spartan UK

Artist Robert Young

Title Great Songs From Great Shows

Record Label EMI UK

Date 1976

Design Feref

Photography Peter Vernon

Artist Ray Conniff His Orchestra & Chorus

Title The Ray Conniff Hi-Fi Companion

Record Label Phillips UK

Date 1960

Artist George Jones

Title Homecoming In Heaven

Record Label Capitol/Stetson Records UK

Date 1962

Artist Dickie Rock & The Miami Showband

Title Dickie Rock & The Miami Showband

Record Label Hallmark/Pickwick UK

Date 1967

"There was a time when the plectrum guitar was often confused with the banjo by the lay public to the eye-brow-raising dispair of devotees off both instruments! This may seem strange today, when every other young man seems to sport a guitar around his neck and prime ministers are as conversant with the names of pop groups as the fans themselves." **Laurie Henshaw**

 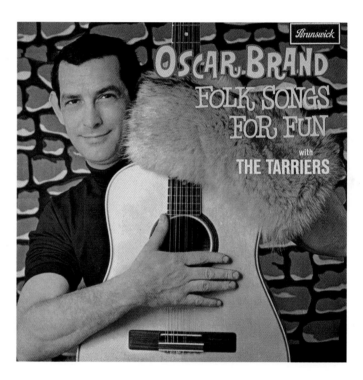

Artist Vincent Bell

Title Pop Goes The Electric Sitar

Record Label Decca US

Date 1968

Photography Hal Buksbaum

Artist Oscar Brand With The Tarriers

Title Folk Songs For Fun

Record Label Brunswick/Decca UK

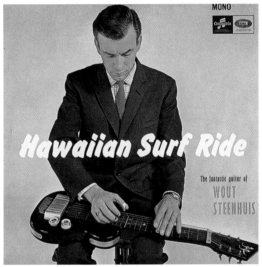

Artist Alfons Bauer

Title Frohe Alpenwanderung

Record Label Die Volks Platte Germany

Artist Wout Steenhuis

Title Hawaiin Surf Ride

Record Label Columbia/EMI

Date 1965

Artist Alfons Bauer

Title Vom Jsartal Zum Tegernsee

Record Label Telefunken Germany

Photography Hans Grimm

Artist Joseph Cooper

Title The World Of Joseph Cooper

Record Label Decca UK

Date 1974

Photography John Thompson

Artist Crazy Otto

Title Crazy Otto Beat

Record Label Polydor UK

Date 1964

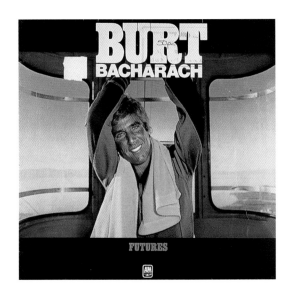

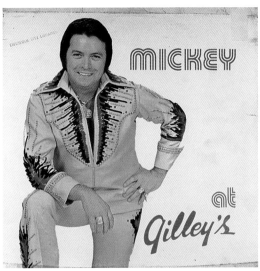

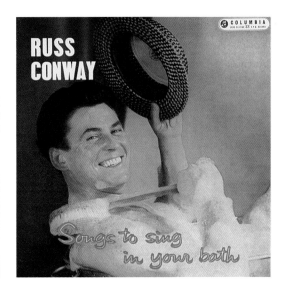

Artist Burt Bacharach	**Artist** Mickey Gilley	**Artist** Russ Conway
Title Futures	**Title** Mickey At Gilley's	**Title** Songs To Sing In Your Bath
Record Label A&M UK	**Record Label** Astro Records US	**Record Label** Columbia/EMI UK
Design Phil Shima	**Date** 1975	**Date** 1959
Photography Kathie McGinty	**Design** Gilley's & Planmark	**Photography** Flair Photography

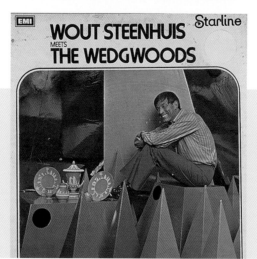

Artist Jack Diamond

Title Jack Diamond 'Live'

Record Label Macle UK

Date 1971

Photography Geoff Baker

Artist Jacinto Antonio

Title La Nueva Onda De Jacinto Antonio

Record Label Caytronics US

Design Jaime Ortiz Pino

Artist Don King

Title Dreams 'n' Things

Record Label Con Brio Records US

Date 1977

Design William George

Photography Jeff Walker

Artist Wout Steenhuis

Title Wout Steenhuis Meets The Wedgewoods

Record Label EMI UK

Date 1971

Photography Fred Warren

Artist Ahvah

Title Aloha From Ahvah Hawaii

Record Label Ahvah Records

Design Honouliuli Graphics

Photography Maurice Mossman

Artist Roger Dee

Title Roger Dee Live

Record Label Toby UK

Artist Various

Title 12 Chart Busters Vol 13

Record Label PYE UK

Date 1974

Artist Giuseppe Di Stefano

Title Di Stefano Operatic Recital

Record Label Decca UK

Date 1959

Artist Hugo Montenegro & His Orchestra

Title The Best Of Hugo Montenegro

Record Label RCA UK

Date 1970

Artist Trevor Crozier & Friends

Title Trouble Over Bridgwater

Record Label One Up/EMI UK

Date 1977

Design Feref

Photography Perter Vernon

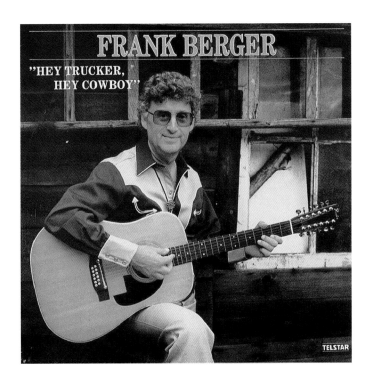

Artist Frank Berger

Title Hey Trucker, Hey Cowboy

Record Label Telstar UK

Artist Justin Wilson

Title How Y'all Are

Record Label Capitol US

Artist Tom & Dick Smothers

Title Golden Hits Of The Smothers Brothers
Vol 2

Record Label Mercury US

Photography Jay Thompson

Artist Rostal & Schaefer

Title Play Two - Piano Favourites

Record Label EMI UK

Date 1976

Artist The Barry Sisters

Title My Mothers Sabbath Candles & Other
Yiddish Songs

Record Label London Records UK

Artist Pam Brody

Title English Muffins & Irish Stew

Record Label BDA Records UK

Date 1974

Design Advertising Associates

Photography Rick Morbey

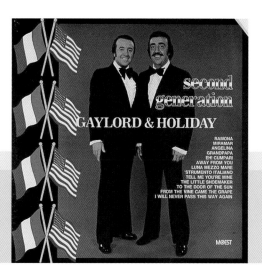

Artist Joe McGrath, Joe Hankinson
& Ginger Dixon

Title Dragon Break

Record Label Pad Records UK

Photography J. Brunskill Associates

Artist Bryan Smith & Brian Dee

Title Side By Side

Record Label Dansan Records UK

Date 1981

Design Dan Galvin

Photography Charles Scott

Artist Gaylord & Holiday

Title Second Generation

Record Label EMI UK

Date 1975

Design Bob Joly

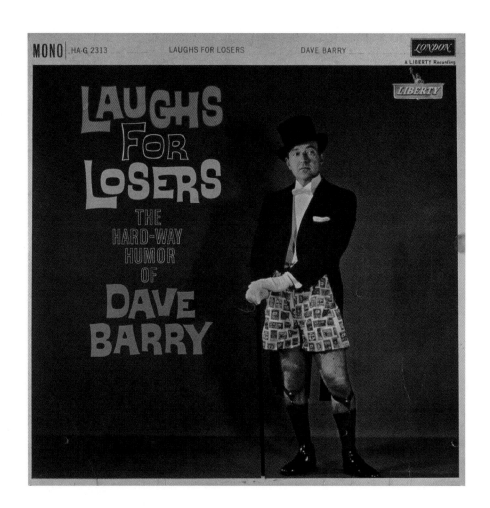

Artist Dave Barry

Title Laughs For Losers

Record Label London Records UK

Design Pate/Francis & Assocaites

Photography Garrett Howard Inc

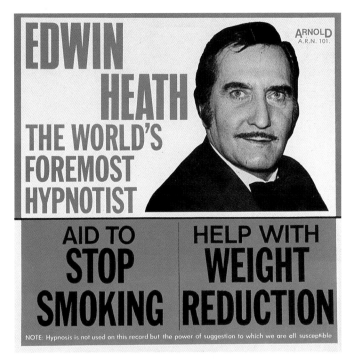

Artist Romark

Title Relax...Your Going To Lose Weight

Record Label Dart Records UK

Date 1974

Design Glen Pierce

Photography Dezo Hoffman

Artist Edwin Heath

Title The Worlds Foremost Hypnotist

Record Label Arnold Records UK

Artist The Dukes Men Of Yale

Title The Dukes Men Of Yale

Date 1963

Photography Fabian Budding

Artist Dutch Swing College

Title The Dutch Swing College On Tour

Record Label Phillips UK

Date 1960

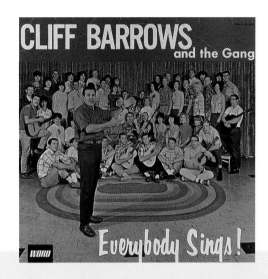

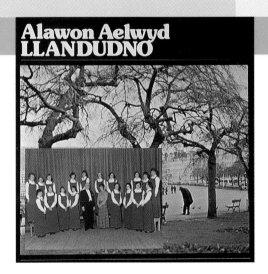

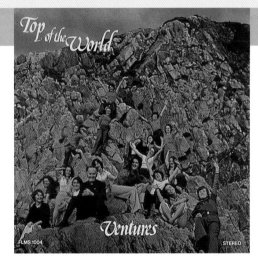

Artist Alawon Aelwyd

Title Llandudno

Record Label Sain Recordiau Wales

Date 1972

Artist Faith Folk

Title Friends

Record Label Wild Dog Records UK

Date 1982

Design Artpoint

Photography Graham Marshment

Artist Ventures

Title Top Of The World

Record Label Flame Records Ireland

Date 1977

Design Tony Johnston

Photography Tony Johnston

Artist Cliff Barrows & The Gang

Title Everybody Sings

Record Label Word Music UK

Date 1973

"This is a collection of real, god - given, anointed prophecies given in the power of the spirit, through the manifestation of the supernatural gift of prophecy. Revealing, startling, amazing, encouraging, uplifting, informing! Ideal to play to groups. It is just like god standing before you and talking to you personally. It is a message from heaven for the christian, preacher and the sinner." **Anon**

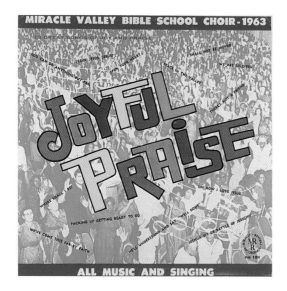

Artist A.A. Allen

Title The Healer Of Broken Hearts

Record Label Miracle Revival Recordings US

Date 1963

Artist Wally Rasmussen & Gospel Singing Family

Title The Full Life Ministry

Record Label Artronics US

Artist Miracle Valley Bible School Choir

Title Joyful Praise

Record Label Miracle Revival Recordings US

Date 1963

Artist A.A. Allen

Title Reach Out And Touch The Lord

Record Label Miracle Revival Recordings US

Date 1964

"Hymn singing - regardless of the scale of its setting - remains an ever meaningful worship experience for every christian. Whether it's a small family gathered around an old upright piano, or a huge congregation flanked by a grand pipe organ and massive choir, the intensity of the expression is of the same high level - hymns offer praise and thanksgiving to god, reflecting man's most spiritual feelings in a triumphant celebration of worship." **Anon**

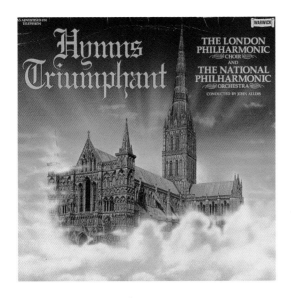 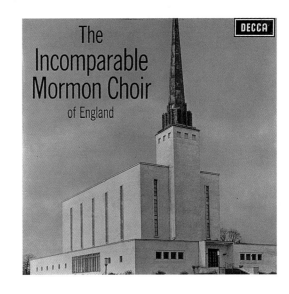

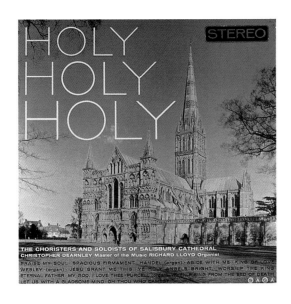 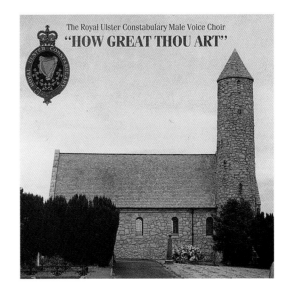

Artist London Philharmonic Choir
Title Hymns Triumphant
Record Label Warwick UK
Date 1984
Design Torchlight

Artist Mormon Choir Of England
Title The Incomparable Mormon Choir Of England
Record Label Decca UK
Date 1966

Artist The Soloists & Choir Of Salisbury Cathdral
Title Holy Holy Holy
Record Label Saga Allied Records UK
Date 1964
Photography John Champion

Artist The Royal Ulster Constabulary Male Voice Choir
Title "How Great Thou Art"
Record Label Window UK
Date 1985
Photography John Johnston

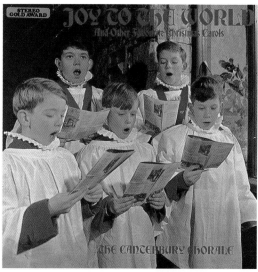

"The spirit of christmas, that intangible feeling that becomes an important part of our lives for just a few days of every year, really springs to life when the songs of christmas are heard. For these much-loved and familiar melodies that form part of our childhood and follow us for the rest of our lives, never lose their appeal. It's an appeal that is as timeless as the very season of goodwill itself." **Anon**

Artist The Jericho Seven

Title Spirituals

Record Label Boulevard UK

Date 1971

Artist The Canterbury Chorale

Title Joy To The World And Other Favourite Christmas Carols

Record Label Stereo Gold Award/PYE UK

Date 1970

Artist Guilford Cathedral Choir

Title Christmas Carols By Guilford Cathedral Choir

Record Label MFP/EMI UK

Date 1966

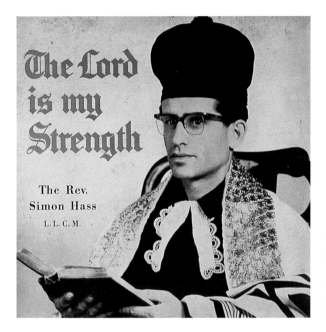

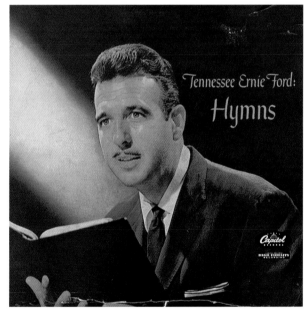

"These great songs of hope and faith have come from the hearts and pens of God-fearing men and women everywhere. There is beauty in melody and strength and power in lyric here that can cause the warrior to lay down his sword, the thief to return his plunder and the sinner to seek forgiveness."
Tennessee Ernie Ford

Artist Rev Simon Hass

Title The Lord Is My Strength

Record Label Lubavitch Foundation UK

Artist Frank Boggs

Title Prayer Of Thanksgiving

Record Label Redemption Records UK

Date 1958

Artist Tennessee Ernie Ford

Title Hymns

Record Label Capitol/EMI UK

Date 1958

Artist Tennessee Ernie Ford

Title Nearer The Cross

Record Label EMI UK

Date 1958

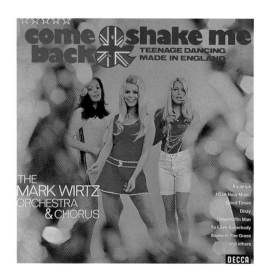

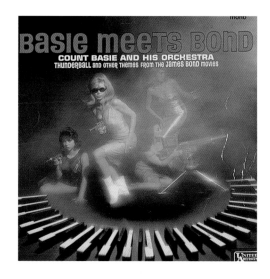

Artist L.A. Sounds Compilation

Title Disco Instrumental

Record Label Chevron Records UK

Date 1979

Artist The Mark Wirtz Orchestra

Title Come Back & Shake Me
Teenage Dancing Made In England

Record Label Decca Germany

Photography J. Dommnich

Artist Count Basie

Title Basie Meets Bond

Record Label United Artists/EMI UK

Date 1966

Artist Los Amigos Del Amambay

Title Music From South America

Record Label Universe US

Date 1961

Artist Various

Title Disco Duniya
Music Indias Disco Sound

Record Label Music India

Date 1982

Artist Morton Gould &
His Symphonic Band

Title Brass and Percussion

Record Label RCA/Victor US

Date 1957

"Disco . . . the most potent force in pop music since the inception of Rock 'n' Roll. Music that has revolutionised the leisure habits of millions throughout the world, the greatest music ever for dancing . . ." **Anon**

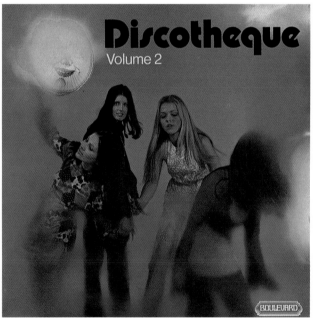

Artist *Various*
Title *Discotheque Vol I*
Record Label *Boulevard UK*
Date *1972*

Artist *Various*
Title *Discotheque Vol 2*
Record Label *Boulevard UK*
Date *1973*

Artist Klaus Wunderlich & Hubert Deuringer

Title We Got Rhythm

Record Label Decca Germany

Artist Zygmunt Jankowski

Title Hammond Pop Party

Record Label Windmill UK

Photography Colour Library International Ltd

"Whether your party is a wild affair where the carpets are rolled up and abandon thrown to the winds, or a sophisticated evening where everyone just sits around to a background of happy music, this record will fill the bill. Just put it on your record - player and see what we mean!" **Anon**

Artist Garry Blake & His Orchestra

Title A Swinging Party

Record Label Columbia/EMI UK

Date 1968

Artist Bing And The Birds

Title Beat Party To The Classics

Record Label Saga UK

Date 1968

Artist Doug Duke

Title Dancing To The Swinging Hammond Organ

Record Label Phillips US

Date 1963

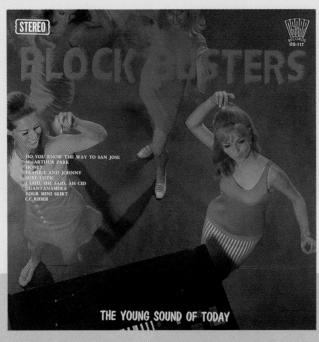

Artist *Various*

Title *Blockbusters*

Record Label *Oscar Records US*

Artist *Various*

Title *Sounds Like Soul*

Record Label *Fontana UK*

Date *1969*

Artist *Big Jim 'H' & His Men Of Rhythm*

Title *Hammond Organ Dance Party*

Record Label *Stereo Gold Award UK*

Date *1971*

Artist *Chaquito*

Title *Magic*

Record Label *Phillips UK*

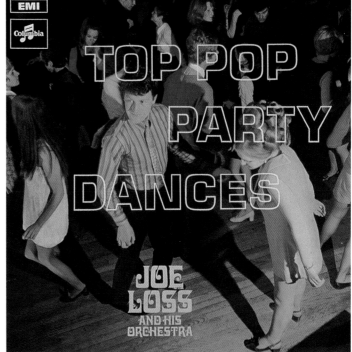

Artist Tommy Kinsman

Title Tommy Kinsman's Swinging Party

Record Label Fontana UK

Date 1964

Artist Joe Loss & His Orchestra

Title Top Pop Party Dances

Record Label Columbia/EMI UK

Date 1969

Artist Albert Decap

Title 16 Super Hits

Record Label Decap Sound Belgium

Artist 101 Strings

Title Italian Hits

Record Label PYE/Golden Guinea US

Artist Various

Title Tranzmusik Für Die Party

Record Label Somerset/Miller International

Germany

Artist Giorgio & Chris

Title Loves In You Loves In Me

Record Label Oasis Records UK

Date 1978

Design Henry Vizcarra

Photography Scott Hensel & Harry Langdon

"In Londons swank Savoy Hotel wild scenes of twisting can be observed. In the magnificent mecca halls half a million dancers a week can be seen twisting, seriously, studiously or happily, according to their bent, and in the salons of ballroom dancing teachers, behind closed doors, people of all walks of life pay many roubles in order to twist to perfection before they perform, albeit casually, at their friend's parties. Films have been made about it, songs have been sung about it, and much money made and spent on it." **Jimmy Savile**

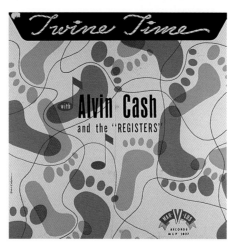

Artist Cyril Stapleton & His Show Band

Title Come Twistin

Record Label Decca UK

Date 1962

Photography Town Magazine

Artist Stanley Black & His Orchestra

Title Dancing In The Dark

Record Label Decca UK

Artist Alvin Cash & The Registers

Title Twine Time

Record Label Mar-v-lus Records US

Design Robert Hoylman

Date 1963

"There was a time back in the middle fifties, when it seemed that Britians dance halls were losing their appeal. The growing interest in television and the increasing popularity of Rock 'n' Roll concerts were just two factors involved in the declining attendance figures - although it's necessary to point out that at no time did the ballroom business hit rock bottom. But times have changed. Over the past few years, both T.V. and Rock 'n' Roll have passed the 'craze' stage and have found a level, and the dance halls are flourishing as never before. Right now, ballrooms are big business once again." **James Wynn**

Artist Sydney Thompson & His Orchestra	**Artist** Joe Loss & His Orchestra	**Artist** Sydney Thompson
Title Dancing To Best Of The Pops	**Title** Party Dance Time No.2	**Title** Star Dancing
Record Label Sydney Thompson Dance	**Record Label** HMV/EMI UK	**Record Label** Sydney Thompson Dance
Records UK	**Date** 1961	Records UK
Date 1972		**Date** 1972

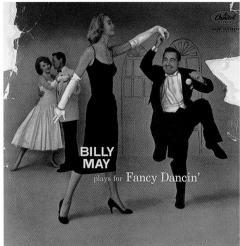

"We predict you'll find this album a delightful and refreshing excursion into a new sound in music! In fact, the newest in sound today! Now is the time, this is the place..." **Anon**

Artist *Marty Portnoy & His Orchestra*	**Artist** *Billy May*	**Artist** *Edmundo & His Orchestra*	**Artist** *Lawrence Welk & His Champagne Music*
Title *Dance Party*	**Title** *Plays For Fancy Dancin*	**Title** *Dancing With Edmundo*	**Title** *Pick-a-Polka*
Record Label *Fidelio UK*	**Record Label** *Capitol US*	**Record Label** *Decca UK*	**Record Label** *Coral US*
		Date *1966*	

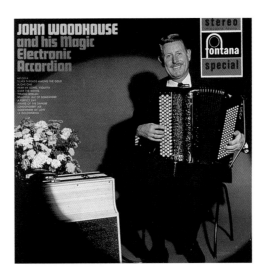

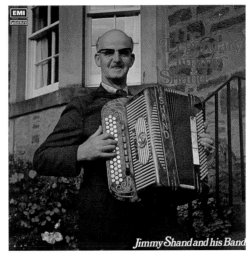

Artist John Woodhouse

Title John Woodhouse & His Magic
Electronic Accordion

Record Label Fontana UK

Date 1967

Artist Harry Hibbs

Title More Harry Hibbs Vol II

Record Label ARC Sound Ltd Canada

Artist Jimmy Shand

Title Jimmy Shand & His Band

Record Label MFP/EMI UK

Date 1975

Artist Jimmy Shand

Title Jimmy Shand & His Band

Record Label Waverley/EMI UK

Date 1968

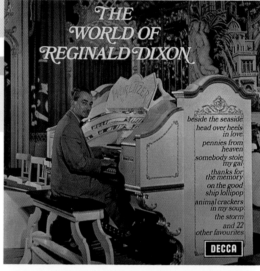

"It is gratifying to see more teenagers taking an interest in organs of all kinds, whereas ten years ago they would opt automatically for electric guitar. Much credit for this must go to the welcome range of home electronic organs on the market, not to mention some excellent teach yourself manuels." **Phil Kelsall**

Artist Phil Kelsall

Title Thank You For The Music

Record Label EMI UK

Date 1978

Design Feref

Photography Henrya Hallas

Artist Reginald Dixon

Title The World Of Reginald Dixon

Record Label Decca UK

Date 1969

Photography Blackpool Tower Co Ltd

Artist Leroy Lewis

Title Panama

Record Label Earsa Records US

Artist Phil Kelsall

Title Meet Me At The Tower

Record Label EMI UK

Date 1982

Design Cream

Photography Henry A. Hallas

"At Fair Grounds the notices say 'The Fair Ground caters for all ages and all classes' - and so it does for he's and she's of all ages and all walks of life, from grandpa who has come with the family, to the toddler who's been promised a ride. The fair means there are things to watch, things to do, things to win and things to try, and there's always something to hear above the hubbub of the crowd. Perhaps it's recorded music or perhaps, if you're lucky, it might even be the real thing - a Fair Organ." **Frank Lee**

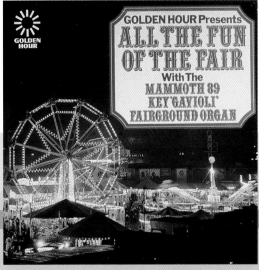

Artist The Gaudin Fair Organ
Title All The Fun Of The Fair
Record Label Joy Records UK
Date 1969
Photography Joseph Siggery

Artist The Gavioli Fair Organ
Title All The Fun Of The Fair
Record Label Golden Hour/PYE UK

Artist Giant Hooghuy Shaharazad
Title Pride Of The Ride In Stereo
Record Label Marble Arch UK
Date 1969
Photography Pat Wood

Artist The Mammoth 'Gavioli' Fair Organ
Title Famous Overtures & Marches
Record Label Decca UK
Date 1968

Artist Norrie Paramor His Strings & Orchestra

Title The Zodiac Suite

Record Label Columbia/EMI UK

"Superb, unusual, outstanding are adjectives too often used, however, as one listens to the swinging cuts from this album all of these immediately come to mind." **Jerry Guiid**

Artist Esquivel & His Orchestra

Title Exploring New Sounds In Hi-Fi

Record Label RCA Victor US

Date 1958

Artist The Three Suns

Title Midnight For Two

Record Label HMV/EMI UK

Date 1957

Artist John Keating

Title Space Experience 2

Record Label EMI UK

Date 1975

Artist Various

Title Constellation

Record Label MFP/EMI UK

Date 1970

Photography Picture Point

Artist John Keating

Title Space Experience

Record Label Columbia/EMI UK

Date 1974

Artist Original Cast Recording

Title Space Is So Startling

Record Label Phillips UK

Date 1963

Artist Eddie Layton

Title Greatest Organ Hits

Record Label Mercury/EMI UK

Date 1961

Artist Russ Garcia

Title Fantastica Music From Outer Space

Record Label Liberty US

Date 1961

Design Garrett - Howard

Artist Jose Jimenez

Title The First Man In Space Jose Jimenez
The Astronaut

Record Label Kapp Canada

Date 1960

Artist Cy Payne, Duffy Power, Victy Silva

Title Disco Round The Moon

Record Label CJMO UK

Date 1978

"What a relief to find imagination at work with a top notch orchestra. Here is a truly refreshing way of treating great hits, each arrangement having a marvellous difference that is both musical and fun. For the pleasures of listening, this album is superb."
Anthony Ascom

"Nelson Riddle deals from a deck that's stacked with a dozen typically brillant arrangements plus a brand new sound . . . one that promises to literally fill your room with dynamic audio excitement." **Anon**

Artist The Liberty Studio Orchestra

Title Tricks With Hits

Record Label Liberty UK

Date 1968

Artist Nelson Riddle & His Orchestra

Title Love Is A Game Of Poker

Record Label Capitol/EMI UK

Date 1962

Photography George Jerman

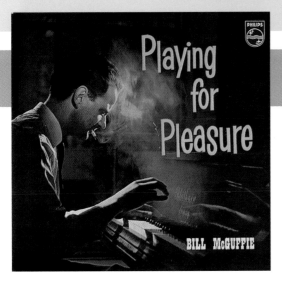

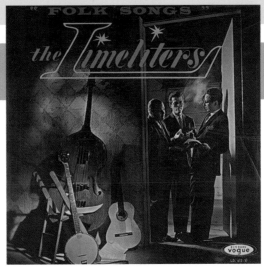

Artist Ann Williams
Title First Time Out
Record Label Summit Records US
Date 1961

Artist Mundell Lowe
Title Blues For A Stripper
Record Label Egmont Records UK
Date 1962
Design Blaise Studio Inc
Photography David Thorpe

Artist Bill McGuffie
Title Playing For Pleasure
Record Label Phillips UK
Date 1961

Artist The Limeliters
Title Folk Songs
Record Label Disques Vogue/Elektra
Records France
Date 1960

Artist *The Three Suns*

Title *Pure Gold*

Record Label *RCA US*

Date *1976*

Artist *Various*

Title *Focus On Phase 4 Stereo*

Record Label *Decca UK*

Date *1968*

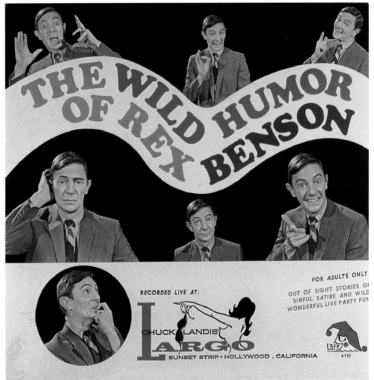

Artist Belle Barth

Title The Book Of Knowledge

Record Label Laff US

Design Sue Mitchell

Artist Rex Benson

Title The Wild Humour Of Rex Benson

Record Label Laff US

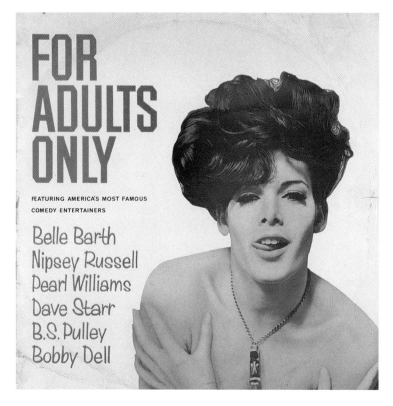

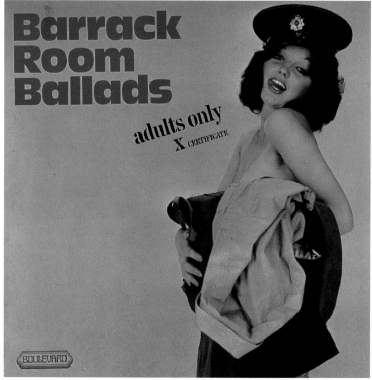

"Gather round, you lovers of lusty lore. All you who have loved and lost, who have loved and won, or who haven't loved at all, prepare yourselves for a trip through the world of requited love. For here is a collection of spicy musical folklore that is bound to whet your emotional appetite and tease your sensibilities." **Anon**

Artist Various

Title For Adults Only

Record Label Surprise Records UK

Artist Various

Title Barrack Room Ballads

Record Label Boulevard UK

Date 1972

"As the art of female impersonation gradually gains the acceptance of the public in general, many impersonators are at last finding the success they deserved all along." **Guy Saville**

Artist Rae Bourbon
Title Ladies Of Burlesque
Record Label UTC US

Artist Lee Sutton
Title A Near 'Miss'
Record Label EMI UK
Date 1968

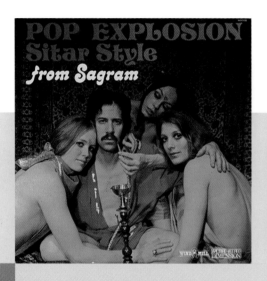

"The Sitar has been an enigma in western eyes and ears. Never has an instrument been able to create a mood so instantly and completely. Just the sound emitted by a cursory running of the fingers across the strings produces strong flashes of oriental mysticism into the mind. So strong in fact, that one can almost smell the heavy perfume of joss sticks in the air." **Anon**

"If you take a look at any album chart anywhere in the world during the past couple of years, you will notice that a new form of music has rapidly been increasing in popularity to the point where it now represents a major side of the record business. That form of music is hard rock. The album contained within this sleeve is a hard rock album." **Anon**

Artist Sagram

Title Pop Explosion Sitar Style

Record Label Windmill UK

Artist The Equinox

Title Hard Rock

Record Label Boulevard UK

Date 1973

Artist Michaelangelo

Title One Voice Many

Record Label Columbia Records UK

Design John Berg

Photography Columbia Records

"The happiest party and dance record you have ever experienced!
Whether you're 19 or 90 here's pure party dynamite" **Anon**

Artist The Gatecrashers

Title Come To Our Surprise Party

Record Label Stereo Gold Award UK

Date 1974

Artist The Gatecrashers

Title Come To Our Surprise Party

Record Label Stereo Gold Award UK

Date 1975

Artist The Gatecrashers

Title Come To Our Surprise Party

Record Label Stereo Gold Award UK

Date 1974

"Obesity . . . is always a bad sign whether it is general or in spots such as the spare tire or heavy thigh, it is never hereditary and rarely a glandular condition. It can almost always be changed."

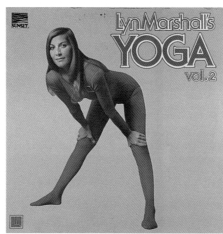

Artist Helen Schifano Sjursen

Title Floor Exercises For Girls & Women

Record Label Hoctor Records US

Date 1965

Photography Judy Cardozo

Artist Lyn Marshall

Title Lyn Marshall's Yoga Vol 2

Record Label Sunset Records UK

Date 1975

Artist Leida Costigan

Title Look Lively Look Lovely With Leida Costigan

Record Label Marble Arch UK

Date 1968

Photography Cyril Stapleton

Artist Bonnie Prudden

Title Keep Fit Be Happy

Record Label Warner Bros US

Photography Charles H. Stewart

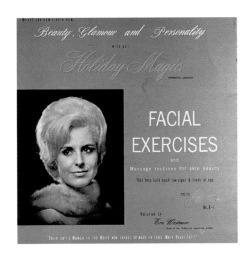

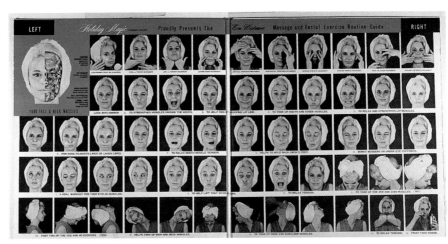

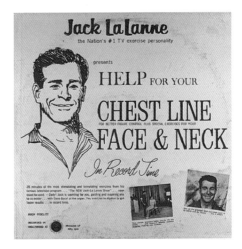

Artist *Ern Westmore*

Title *Facial Exercises & Massage Routines*

For Skin Beauty

Record Label *Holiday Magic UK*

Artist *Jack La Lance*

Title *Help For Your Chestline, Face & Neck*

Record Label *Commercial Sound Records US*

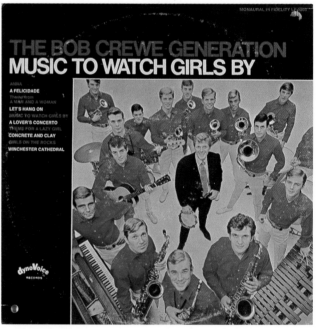

Artist Pat Williams

Title Shades Of Today

Record Label Verve/MGM UK

Date 1968

Design Jack Anesh

Photography Timothy Galfas

Artist The Bob Crewe Generation

Title Music To Watch Girls By

Record Label Dyno Voice Records US

Date 1967

Design Forlenza-Venosa Associates

Photography Ron Harris

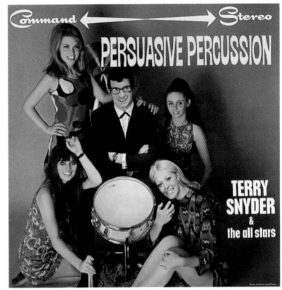

Artist Kevin Gavin

Title Hey This Is Kevin Gavin

Record Label Parker Records US

Design Blaise Studio Inc

Photography Jerry Dieter

Artist Terry Snyder & The All Stars

Title Persuasive Percussion

Record Label Command Records US

Date 1965

Design Josef Albers

Photography Anthony Lloyd-Parker

Artist John Baldry

Title Long John Baldry & The Hoochie
Coochie Men

Record Label Hallmark/Pickwick UK

Date 1965

Artist Chris Montez

Title The More I See You. Call Me

Record Label PYE UK

Date 1966

Design Peter Whorf Graphics

Photography Fred Poore

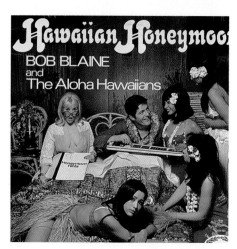

Artist *Santa Esmeralda*

Title *Don't Let Me Be Misunderstood*

Record Label *Phillips France*

Artist *Johnnie Gray & The Reg Tilsley Orchestra*

Title *Full House Saxes*

Record Label *Fontana UK*

Date *1968*

Photography *Henri Seinier & Co*

Artist *Bob Blaine & The Aloha Hawaiins*

Title *Hawaiin Honeymoon*

Date *1969*

Record Label *Hallmark UK*

Artist *Batchelors*

Title *Girls*

Record Label *Decca UK*

Date *1966*

Design *Decca Publicity Art*

Photography *Decca Publicity Art*

Artist *Herb Alpert & The Tijuana Brass*

Title *Going Places*

Record Label *A&M UK*

Artist *The Ritchie Family*

Title *The Ritchie Family*

Record Label *Mercury UK*

Date *1979*

Design *Jack Morali*

Photography *Dick Zimmerman*

"From the brilliant and scintillating percussive effects that depict the busy bazaars in Bagdad to the sensuous woodwinds that take us to the forbidden halls of the temple dancers - these are the moods and sounds that portray the fascinating ports and places of our sojourn in music. From the tent harems of Arab Dance to the nostalgic loveliness of Song of India, this brilliant high fidelity is your passport to adventure and romance East Of Suez." **Anon**

Artist London Philharmonic Orchestra

Title Bolero

Record Label PYE/Golden Guinea UK

Date 1959

Artist 101 Strings

Title East Of Suez

Record Label Budget Sound Inc US

"This package now lets you join the trend toward "The Now" way of sensual living. Your mate's first reaction may be one of shock! But he'll be purring real soon. Ladies, show him how liberated you are, show him everything you want. Imagine the effect and control you can have on that certain someone. With this package, you can tease him, and please him. As you bump and grind, he'll lose his mind...to you. You will undoubtedly find yourself much more appreciated and in fact, in demand. We promise that you will have a very memorable time, and of course so will he." **Anon**

Artist The Sultans Caravan
Title Belly Dance To Great Navel Music
Record Label RCA US
Design Craig De Camps
Design Acy Lehman

Artist Sonny Lester & His Orchestra
Title How To Belly Dance For Your Husband
Record Label Emus US

Artist Teddy Phillips & His Orchestra
Title Music To Strip For Your Man By
Record Label ALA US
Photography Robert Wotherspoon

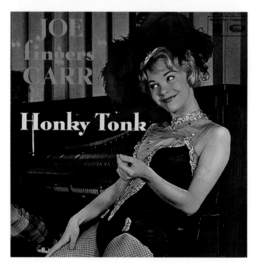

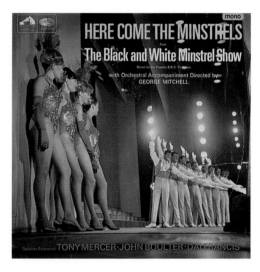

"Feather Boa's, knee length beads, raccoon coats, vamps and sheiks, supercharged cars and illlicit stills - all went to make up the gay, mad, 'roaring twenties'. A 'Back-to-the-twenties movement in dress is already well under way, the most 'with it'' mods now looking like their mothers and fathers did in those dim and dusty pictures. The Music too has a new and fresh appeal to the youth of today and, for once, their mums and dads don't want them to turn down the volume for this remains their music too, the sounds to which they boop-a-dooped through their own younger days." **Anon**

Artist Harry Breuer & Orchestra

Title The Happy Sound Of Ragtime

Record Label Audio Fidelity US

Date 1960

Artist David Carroll & His Orchestra

Title Percussion Parisienne

Record Label EMI UK

Date 1961

Artist Joe 'Fingers' Carr

Title Honky Tonk

Record Label MFP/EMI UK

Date 1959

Design Wendy Bray

Photography Shelley Graphics

Artist The Black & White Minstrels

Title Here Come The Minstrels

Record Label EMI UK

Date 1966

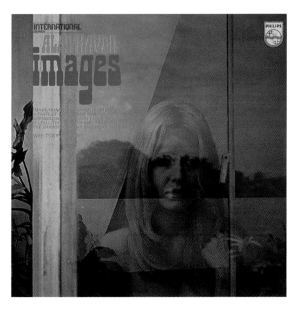

Artist Alan Haven

Title Images

Record Label Phillips UK

Date1974

Artist Various

Title Out Of The Blue

Record Label CBS UK

Date1973

"How often do we hear a song from the past and remember somebody we shared it with; was it a visit to a show, film or possibly driving along in a car with the radio on? We associate it with an event and almost always with the artist we first heard perform it. The wonderful thing about LP recordings is the ability of being able to collect these occasions into permanent memories. Some people collect scrap albums, photography albums and some collect records, to hear once again songs that gave us infinite pleasure in the past." **Anon**

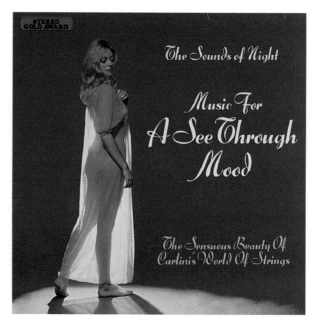

Artist Gordon Jenkins His Orchestra
& The Ralph Brewster Singers
Title Night Dreams
Record Label Capitol US
Photography Ken Whitmore

Artist Carlini's World Of Strings
Title Music For A See Through Mood
Record Label Stereo Gold Award UK
Date 1971
Photography Paul Chave

"Let's be honest about it. This is a mood music album. It has piano and strings and some great ballads from the halcyon years of song. It's designed to put you and your loved one in the right mood while dancing cheek to cheek. That's what mood music is all about!" **Arthur Jackson**

Artist Nadezhda Babkina

Title Popular Russian Folk Songs

Record Label Meloodia USSR

Date 1983

Design V. Alexandrov

Photography A. Zmulukin

Artist Mr Osborne

Title The Romantic Mr Osborne, his Piano & Orchestra

Record Label Rediffusion UK

Date 1973

Design Stephen Hill Design Services

Artist The Four Freshmen

Title The Four Freshmen Sing

Record Label Crown UK

Date 1970

Artist The Columbia Musical Treasuries Orchestra

Title Sugar & Spice

Record Label Columbia Record Club US

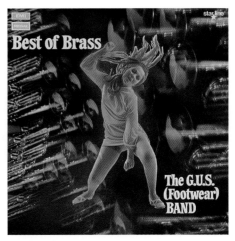

Artist *The Button Down Brass*

Title *Lets Be Gay With The Button Down Brass*

Record Label *Fontana UK*

Date *1968*

Artist *The George Shearing Quintet With Brass Choir*

Title *Burnished Brass*

Record Label *Captiol US*

Artist *The Border Brass*

Title *The Sweet Sounds Of Tijuana*

Record Label *Stereo Gold Award/PYE UK*

Artist *The G.U.S (Footwear) Band*

Title *Best Of Brass*

Record Label *Regal/EMI UK*

Date *1969*

Artist *The Button Down Brass*

Title *Featuring The Funky Trumpet Of Ray Davies*

Record Label *Fontana UK*

Date *1968*

Artist Various
Title Out Of Sight
Record Label Design Records US

"Any mention of swinging London automatically brings to mind dolly Mini-Skirted girls, lively discotheques and Carnaby Street. But there's a lot more to the swinging capital than just those attractions. Music for a start. The kind of music that keeps the ear drums pounding in discotheques and adds weekly excitement to the nation's pop charts." **Anon**

Artist The Peter Thomas Sound Orchestra	**Artist** The London Philharmonic Orchestra	**Artist** James Last Band
Title Organic	**Title** Swinging London	**Title** Thats Life
Record Label Polydor UK	**Record Label** Stereo Gold Award/PYE UK	**Record Label** Polydor UK
Date 1968	**Date** 1970	**Date** 1967

STEREO UAS 6647
LONDON BY GEORGE
GEORGE MARTIN
AND HIS ORCHESTRA

WINCHESTER CATHEDRAL
WHITER SHADE OF PALE
SGT. PEPPER'S LONELY HEARTS CLUB BAND
TO SIR, WITH LOVE
ALFIE
THEME ONE
HOLE IN MY SHOE
I AM THE WALRUS
ITCHYCOO PARK
ELEPHANTS AND CASTLES
KING'S ROAD RASPBERRY PARADE
FROST OVER LONDON

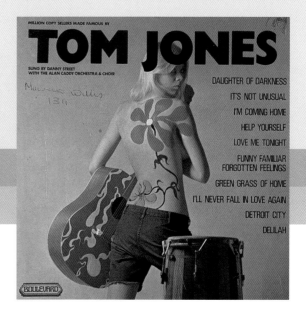

MILLION COPY SELLERS MADE FAMOUS BY
TOM JONES
SUNG BY DANNY STREET
WITH THE ALAN CADDY ORCHESTRA & CHOIR

DAUGHTER OF DARKNESS
IT'S NOT UNUSUAL
I'M COMING HOME
HELP YOURSELF
LOVE ME TONIGHT
FUNNY FAMILIAR FORGOTTEN FEELINGS
GREEN GRASS OF HOME
I'LL NEVER FALL IN LOVE AGAIN
DETROIT CITY
DELILAH

BOULEVARD

EUROPA
Love is Blue

Lady Madonna
Hadin' Home
u.a.m.

Blooming Hits
PAUL MAURIAT
and his orchestra

PHILIPS

Featuring
LOVE IS BLUE
(L'AMOUR EST BLEU)

STEREO
PLAYABLE MONO

PENNY LANE
THIS IS MY SONG
(THERE'S A) KIND OF HUSH
MAMA
SOMETHIN' STUPID
PUPPET ON A STRING
INCH ALLAH
L'AMOUR EST BLEU (LOVE IS BLUE)
SEULS AU MONDE (ALONE IN THE WORLD)
ADIEU A LA NUIT (ADIEU TO THE NIGHT)
TA, TA, TA, TA
L'IMPORTANT C'EST LA ROSE

PHILIPS

"With the 'Youth Plosion' taking place around the world, the late 1960's finds young people creating exciting new trends in the arts and music. Fresh new sounds from electric guitars, swinging organs, Indian Sitar and all sorts of percussion instruments and electronic sounds to create the moods of beat and psychedelia. These sounds are the reflection of the restless new generation of people in their teens and twenties - sounds and songs of the now generation." **Anon**

Artist George Martin & His Orchestra
Title London By George
Record Label United Artists US
Date 1968

Artist Danny Street With The Alan Caddy Orchestra & Choir
Title Million Copy Sellers Made Famous By Tom Jones
Record Label Boulevard UK
Date 1971

Artist 101 Strings, The Spots & The Petards
Title Love Is Blue
Record Label Europa Germany
Date 1969

Artist Paul Mauriat & His Orchestra
Title Blooming Hits
Record Label Phillips UK
Date 1967

Artist Wild Cherry

Title Electrified Funk

Record Label Epic UK

Date 1977

Design Ed Lee

Photography Frank Lafitte

Artist Harry Stoneham

Title The Very Best Of Harry Stoneham

Record Label EMI UK

Date 1974

Photography Spectrum Colour Library

Artist Lemon

Title Lemon

Record Label CBS UK

Date 1978

Design Ancona Design

Photography Bernard Atelier Vidal

Artist Sticky Fingers

Title Sticky Fingers

Record Label Epic/CBS US

Date 1978

Design Ancona Design Atelier

Photography Bernard Vidal

'Black is Beautiful'

YOU CAN DO MAGIC · COULD IT BE I'M FALLING IN LOVE
THE LOVE I LOST · BROTHER LOUIE · GHETTO CHILD
LIKE SISTER AND BROTHER · SMARTY PANTS · LOVE TRAIN
HELP ME MAKE IT THROUGH THE NIGHT · DOCTOR MY EYES
FEEL THE NEED IN ME · GONNA MAKE YOU AN OFFER YOU CAN'T REFUSE

SPECTRO-STEREO
DIMENSION

WIND MILL

Artist Unoriginal Artists
Title Black Is Beautiful
Record Label Windmill UK
Date 1974

  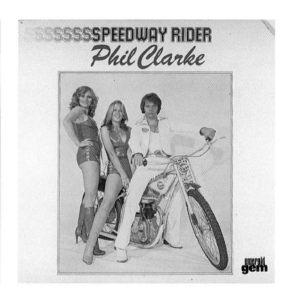

Artist The Shangri-Las

Title Leader Of The Pack

Record Label Red Bird/PYE UK

Date 1965

Artist Harry Stoneham

Title High Power Hammond

Record Label Columbia/EMI UK

Date 1970

Photography Alan Willmouth

Artist Phil Clarke

Title Speedway Rider

Record Label Emerald/Decca UK

Date 1978

Photography George Smith

Sensation Rag (Quickstep)

Tea For Two Cha Cha

Tico Tico (Samba)

A Pretty Girl Is Like A
Melody (Foxtrot)

South Rampart St. Parade (Quickstep)

Charleston

La Cumparsita (Tango)

Ko-Ko-Mo (Rock)

Patricia (Baion)

S'Wonderful (Quickstep)

So Blue (Waltz)

I Wonder Where My Baby
Is Tonight (Charleston)

El Choclo (Tango)

Tenderly (Foxtrot)

Perfidia (Cha Cha)

When You Wore A Tulip (Quickstep)

FULL-RANGE
Embassy
HIGH-FIDELITY

"They're young, very much in love and they're all set for their first dance date together. Yes, a real swinging evening lies ahead. In terms of money it will cost them little, but they'll derive more pleasure from this evening than they would from an expensive night out at the most exclusive night club.

So off they go, with their eyes sparkling and their feet a-tapping. At the dance hall, the band is really letting rip with Rock 'n' Roll, the Latin-American beat of the cha cha, the soft, soothing strains of the Waltz (to allow them to get their breath back after that hectic rock number), and then the dance that mum and dad did some 25 years ago but which they now claim as their own, yes - the Charleston. All too soon, the night is over, and two tired but very happy and starry eyed teenagers make their way home. Yes, the night is over for them - until the next time." **Anon**

Artist Various	**Artist** Reg Owen & His Orchestra
Title Dance Date	**Title** Get Happy
Record Label Embassy Records UK	**Record Label** Palette US
Date 1961	

"A wisp of cigarette smoke in the soft lamplight, the tinkle of a glass, a hushed whisper . . . and music for lovers only." **Anon**

Artist Jackie Gleason

Title Music For Lovers Only

Record Label Capitol US

Artist Bill Snyder

Title Music For Holding Hands

Record Label Brunswick/Decca UK

Date 1958

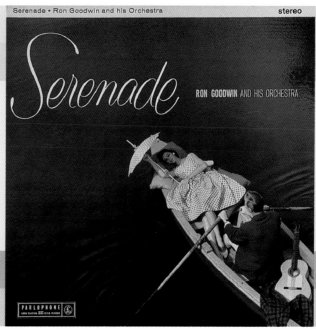

"All the songs in this album characterise the different moods and feelings of love. And why shouldn't we immerse ourselves in love? Together with music, the international language, love can be expressed with no barriers of misunderstanding. Therefore, love and music are two delights in life which all of us can enjoy, all over the world." **Ivor Raymonde**

Artist The Mike Sammes Singers
Title And I Love You So
Record Label EMI UK
Date 1974
Design Geoff Hocking
Photography Geoff Hocking

Artist Ron Goodwin & His Orchestra
Title Serenade
Record Label Parlophone/EMI UK
Date 1961

"For anyone who wants the most romantic of mood music, this is it. The titles, as well as the melodies, are redolent with glamour; the songs are those to which lovers have always thrilled; there are tender heart beats in every bar." **Anon**

Artist Lenny Dee	**Artist** Nelson Riddle & His Orchestra	**Artist** Nelson Riddle & His Orchestra	**Artist** Nino Nanni
Title Something Special	**Title** Hey Let Yourself Go	**Title** C'mon Get Happy	**Title** Chic To Chic
Record Label Brunswick/Decca UK	**Record Label** Capitol US	**Record Label** Capitol US	**Record Label** Carlton US
Photography Hal Buksbaum	**Photography** Alex De Paola		

"No experience can match the emotional joys of two people alone. The moments when two become one on the island of love. The quiet hours - the intimate hours when nothing matters in the world outside. Soft light on darkness for this special mood enchanced by unobtrusive music, music that speaks of warmth and intimacy. The velvet rich tones of strings and delicate caress of woodwinds. These are moments when only gentle rain is heard on passages of soft erotic rhythm pulsating to a background of violence. These are the sounds of night." **Anon**

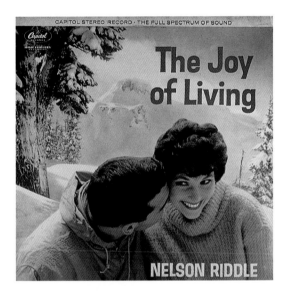

Artist Nelson Riddle	**Artist** Norrie Paramor & His Orchestra	**Artist** The Melachrino Strings & Orchestra	**Artist** Donny L
Title The Joy Of Living	**Title** Lovers In Latin	**Title** Music For Dining	**Title** Once More With Feeling
Record Label Capitol US	**Record Label** EMI UK	**Record Label** RCA Victor US	**Record Label** Epitome US
Date 1959	**Date** 1959	**Date** 1958	**Date** 1977

"May we suggest that you paste a wedding announcement in this space and present this album as a gift to the bride and groom." **Anon**

Artist 101 Strings

Title A Bridal Boquet

Record Label Somerset Records US

"There is a special flavour about continental songs, like continental food and wine, there is something vaguely exotic about them. They match up with the Englishman's idea of Italians and Frenchmen, sophisticated, debonair and romantic. The love songs of France and Italy, whatever the reason, have a special place in our affections. It might simply be that they have such unforgettable melodies. You will never have heard them more splendidly or richly sung and presented than on this present disc. c'est magnifique." **Anon**

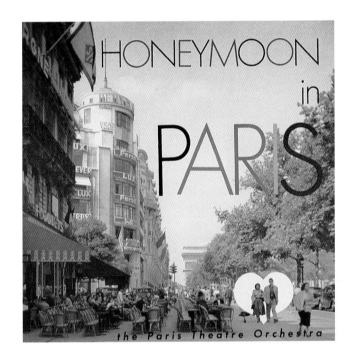

Artist The Paris Theatre Orchestra

Title Honeymoon In Paris

Record Label PYE/Golden Guinea UK

Date 1959

Artist Renato Carosone His Piano & Quartetto

Title Honeymoon In Rome

Record Label Capitol US

Photography Pan Am World Airways

Artist Joan & Ted

Title Joan & Ted

Record Label Allegro Records UK

Artist Carole Gordon & Bob Newman

Title In Harmony

Record Label Together Records UK

Design Carole & Bob

Photography Kenneth Edwards

Artist Paul Weston

Title Music For The Fireside

Record Label The World Record Club Ltd UK

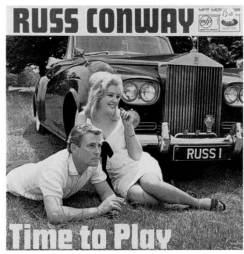

Artist Steve Lawrence & Eydie Gormé

Title We Got Us

Record Label The World Record Club Ltd UK

Photography Gary Wagner

Artist Russ Conway

Title Time To Play

Record Label Music For Pleasure Ltd/EMI UK

Date 1966

Photography Edgar Brind

Artist Merv & Merla

Title Windborne

Record Label Word Ltd UK

Date 1973

Artist Various

Title Famous Operatic Arias With Famous Stars

Record Label Hollywood Records US

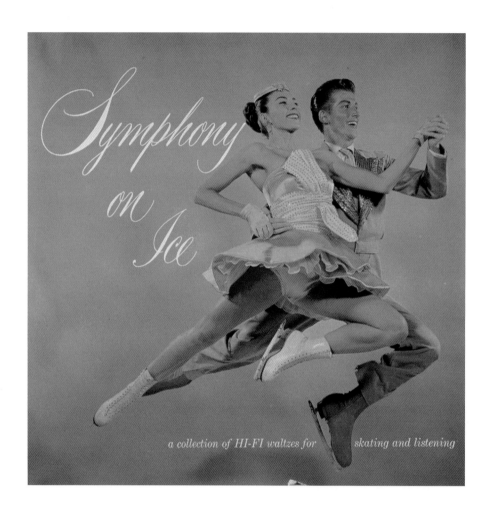

Symphony
on Ice

a collection of HI-FI waltzes for skating and listening

Artist *The Kingsway Strings*

Title *A Symphony On Ice*

Record Label *PYE Golden Guinea UK*

Date *1958*

Photography *Holiday On Ice*

Artist *Original Sound Recording*
Title *Law ' You & Divorce*
Record Label *Law-U-Records US*
Date *1968*
Design *Dad Rica*
Photography *Ken Gale*

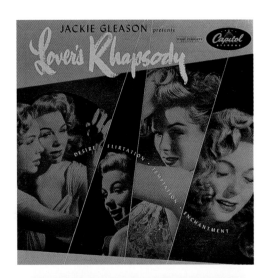

"Girls names are funny things. You instinctively like some of them; you just as instinctively dislike others. Basically, you'll find it's a conditioning process. If there happened to be an overbearing girl in grade school who used to make fun of you and embarrass you, chances are you'll never like the name she went by. On the other hand, if you happen to have had a wonderful older cousin who used to come around regularly and take you out driving in her car and buy you ice cream cones, you'll more than likely to this day be in love with her name. In a sense, you might say, girls names set moods, just as certain types of music do." **George T. Simon**

Artist Jackie Gleason	**Artist** Various	**Artist** Jackie Gleason	**Artist** The Mikes Sammes Session	**Artist** The Melachrino Orchestra
Title Lover's Rhapsody	**Title** Background Music - Songs We	**Title** Music To Remember Her	**Title** Sammes Session	**Title** The Immortal Ladies
Record Label Capital US	Remember	**Record Label** Capitol US	**Record Label** The World Record Club UK	**Record Label** RCA/Victor US
Photography Sid Avery	**Record Label** Capitol US		**Date** 1965	**Date** 1956
	Date 1952			

"Of the innumerable things that may evoke memories of a girl from perfume to laughter to a clear, bright shade of lipstick - there is nothing so thoroughly, so absorbingly evocative as music. With a particularly vivid poignancy a familiar melody can call to mind a certain girl in many, many past events, in many, many moods." **Anon**

Artist The Roy Cliffs

Title Music For Relaxing

Record Label Hollywood Records US

Artist Fran Warren

Title Hey There Here's Fran Warren

Record Label Gala Records UK

Date 1959

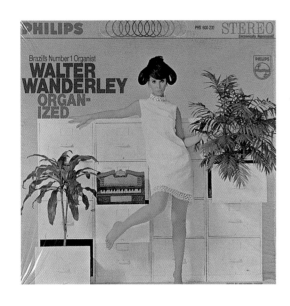

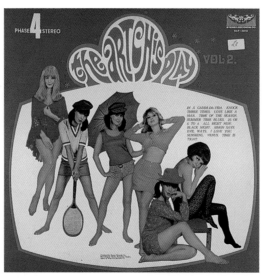

Artist Walter Wanderley

Title Organ-ized

Record Label Phillips US

Artist The Artchis Play

Title The Artchis Play Vol 2

Record Label Phase Four Stereo UK

Artist Lee Akers & The Electric Generation

Title Heavy, Heavy, Heavy

Record Label Crown US

Artist The Generation Gap

Title Up Up & Away

Record Label Custom US

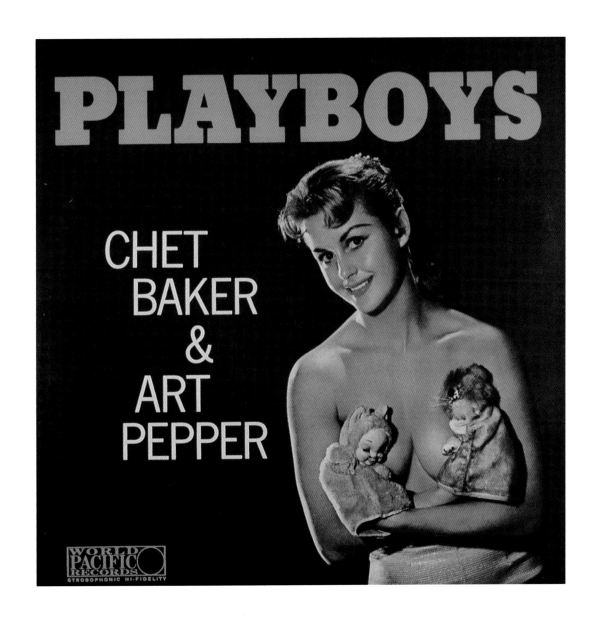

Artist *The Chet Baker & Art Pepper Sextet*

Title *Playboys*

Record Label *World Pacific Records US*

Date *1957*

Design *Chuck Hyman*

Photography *Peter Gowland*

Artist Herb Alperts Tijuana Brass

Title Whipped Cream & Other Delights

Record Label PYE UK

Date 1965

Design Peter Whorf Graphics

Artist The Amazing Dancing Band Vol 2

Title These Boots Are Made For Dancin'

Record Label Verve/MGM UK

Date 1968

Artist Alfred Scholz & His Silver Strings

Title Music For The Small Hours

Record Label Deacon Records UK

Date 1971

Artist The Golden Leaves

Title A Love Affair With The Golden Leaves

Record Label London Records/Decca UK

Date 1967

Design Ralph Moore Morris

Artist Orquestra Cristobal Chaves

Title Tropical Fire

Record Label Regal/EMI UK

Date 1967

Artist Chaquito

Title Chaquito & The Quedo Brass

Record Label Fontana UK

Date 1967

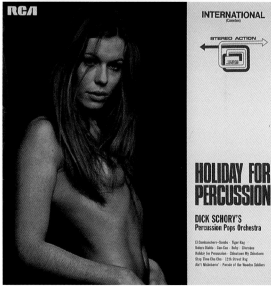

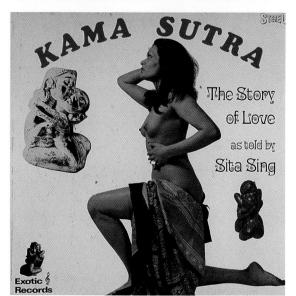

"Blush not, you timid souls who have not steeped yourselves in the joys of love, for in these strains you will find much to pique the imagination. Shrink not, you cautious ones who pride yourselves on following the straight and narrow path. Scoff not, you sophisticates who think you have heard everything there is to hear. For in these recorded ballads you will hear some of the most famous ditties of all time - epics of love unchained, ribald lyrics cast in the mold of the immortal boccaccio, bone tickling songs of jaded women, conniving men and head strong lasses." **Anon**

Artist Various

Title Music To Bathe By

Record Label CBS US

Artist Love On Love

Title Love On Love

Record Label Power Exchange Records UK

Date 1976

Design Picture Palace

Photography Roman Salicki

Artist Dick Schory's Percussion Pops Orchestra

Title Holiday For Percussion

Record Label RCA UK

Date 1970

Photography Eric Howard

Artist Sita Sing

Title Kama Sutra The Story Of Love Told By Sita Sing

Record Label Exotic Records US

Photography Ron Howard

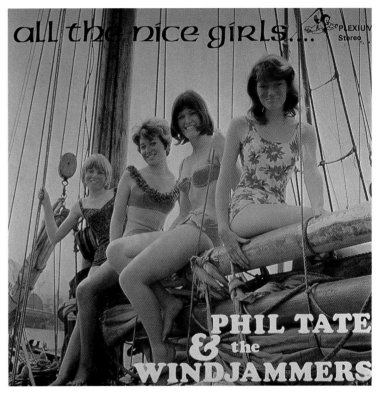

Artist Various

Title Stereo Parade (A New Look In Sound)

Record Label Polydor UK

Date 1962

Artist Phil Tate & The Windjammers

Title All The Nice Girls

Record Label Plexium Records UK

"The subtly shifting rhythmic accents, the changing moods, the facile, switching from jazz to mambo, from baiao to jazz, the piquant exotic flavouring provided by the percussion - all these factors combine to form an album of outstanding originality and distinction." **Anon**

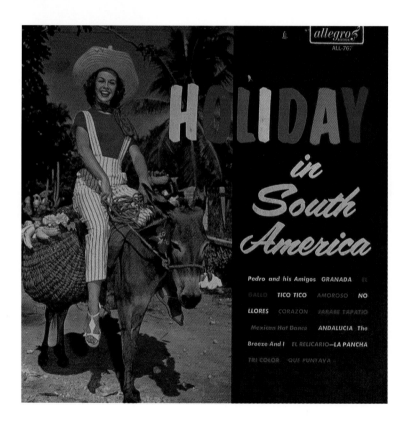

Artist Cees Verschoor & Dolf Van Der Linden Orchestra
Title Dutch Sax
Record Label Capitol US
Photography Paul Huf

Artist Michel René & His Orchestra
Title Strings In The Enchanted Garden
Record Label Hollywood US

Artist Pedro & His Amigos
Title Holiday In South America
Record Label Allegro/Pickwick UK
Date 1965

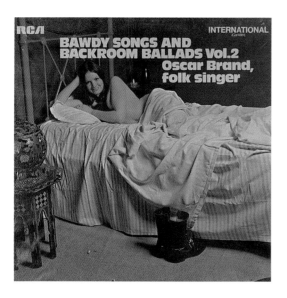

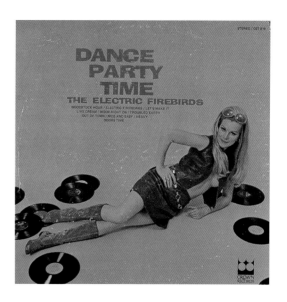

Artist Oscar Brand

Title Bawdy Songs & Backroom Ballads Vol 2

Record Label RCA International UK

Date 1970

Artist Kelso Hersten Et Ses Guitares

Title Les Grands Airs De Films Western

Record Label Mode Disques France

Photography Bianchini

Artist The Electric Firebirds

Title Dance Party Time

Record Label Crown Records US

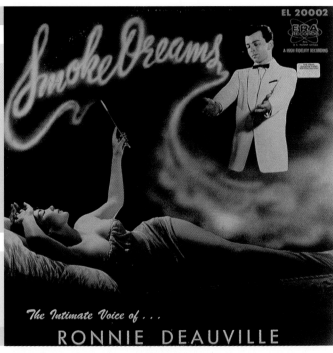

"So lie back and prepare for an experience. In these times of transitionary pleasures it is good to have music that sets a mood of deep feeling. A feeling that is evoked time and time again. Something that is appreciated more and more with each playing." **Anon**

Artist Eddie Barclay & His Dance Orchestra

Title Music For Dreaming

Record Label Felsted Records UK

Artist Ronnie Deauville

Title Smoke Dreams

Record Label ERA Records US

Design Phil Howard

Photography Dusty Rhodes

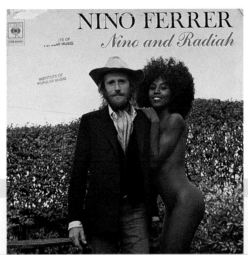

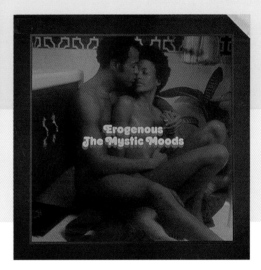

Artist Cerrone
Title Love In C Minor
Record Label Atlantic UK
Date 1976
Photography G. Spitzer

Artist Nino Ferrer & Radiah Frye
Title Nino & Radiah
Record Label CBS UK
Date 1973
Photography Richard Bennett

Artist James Gilstrap
Title Love Talk
Record Label Chelsea UK
Date 1976
Design Linda Dietrich

Artist Hot R.S.
Title Forbidden Fruit
Record Label Contagious Music Brasil
Date 1979
Design Donald Dallas
Photography Pieter De Ras

Artist Erogenous
Title The Mystic Moods
Record Label Mint/Decca UK
Date 1976
Design William S. Harvey
Photography Peter D'Aprix

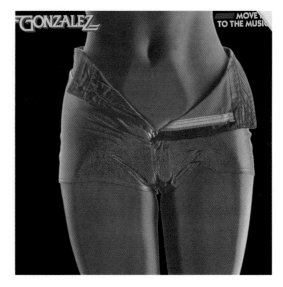

Artist Silver Convention

Title Discotheque Vol 1

Record Label Magnet Records UK

Date 1975

Design Ken Ley

Artist Silver Convention

Title Discotheque Vol 2

Record Label Magnet Records UK

Date 1976

Design Ken Ley, Magnet Records

Artist Gonzalez

Title Move To The Music

Record Label Sidewalk UK

Date 1979

Design Cream

Photography Jerome Ducrot

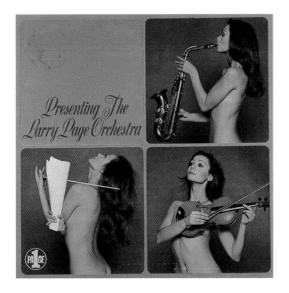

"Middle Of The Road music falls between the categories of out-and-out pop music and pop of a 'heavier' nature. Its main function is that of late-night listening or a background to everyday activities. Over the last few years it has become increasingly popular with record buyers who've wanted to get away from the music the more pop-orientated radio programmes produce." **Ian Middleton**

Artist The Larry Page Orchestra
Title Presenting The Larry Page Orchestra
Record Label Page One Records UK

Artist Ken Morrish
Title Hammond Party Time
Record Label MFP/EMI UK
Date 1970
Design Jack Wood
Photography Pictorial Press

Artist Sounds Nice
Title Love At First Sight
Record Label Rare Earth/Motown US
Date 1970
Design Curtis McNair & Tom Schlesinger
Photography Hendin

Artist Middle Of The Road
Title Music For Coming & Going
Record Label Decca UK
Date 1973
Photography Suzette Stephens

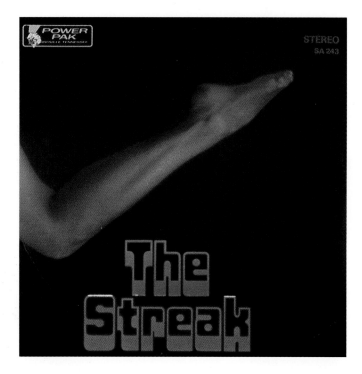

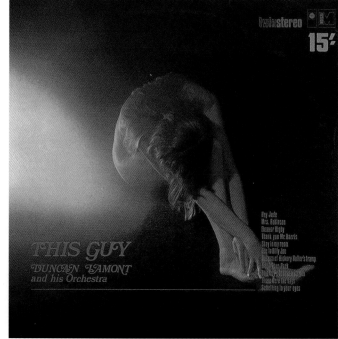

Artist Various

Title The Streak

Record Label Gusto US

Artist Duncan Lamont & His Orchestra

Title This Guy

Record Label Morgan Records UK

Photography James Torney

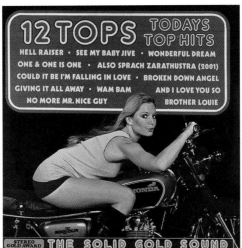

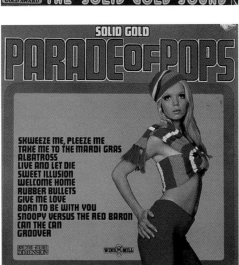

"Top Of The Pops sounds while they are hot on the BBC charts. The original hit sounds that are selling millions. Look for an exciting new album of up to date hits each month. Build the most exciting collection of pop tunes in your neighbourhood." **Anon**

Artist Unoriginal Artists
Title The Original Sounds Of 12 Tops
Record Label Stereo Gold Award

Artist Unoriginal Artists
Title The Original Sounds Of 12 Tops
Record Label Stereo Gold Award UK

Artist Unoriginal Artists
Title The Original Sounds Of 12 Tops
Record Label Stereo Gold Award UK

Artists Unoriginal Artists
Title Solid Gold Parade Of Pops
Record Label Windmill UK
Date 1973

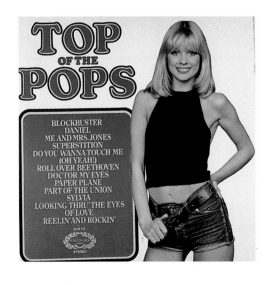

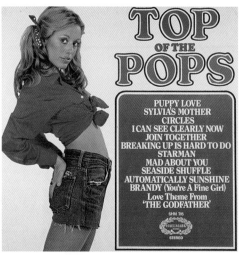

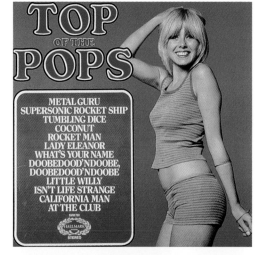

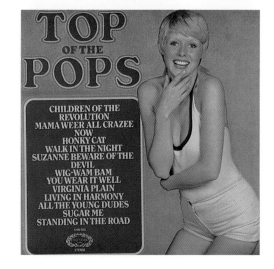

Artist Unoriginal Artists

Title Top Of The Pops

Record Label Hallmark/Pickwick UK

Date 1973

Artist Unoriginal Artists

Title Top Of The Pops

Record Label Hallmark/Pickwick UK

Date 1972

Artist Unoriginal Artists

Title Top Of The Pops

Record Label Hallmark/Pickwick UK

Date 1972

Artist Unoriginal Artists

Title Top Of The Pops

Record Label Hallmark/Pickwick UK

Date 1972

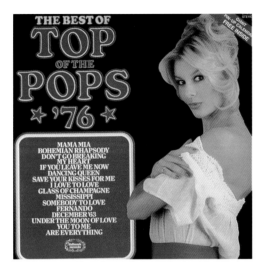

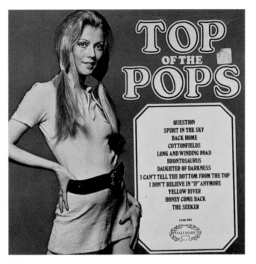

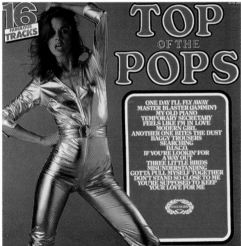

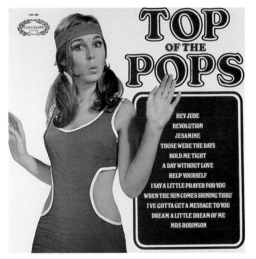

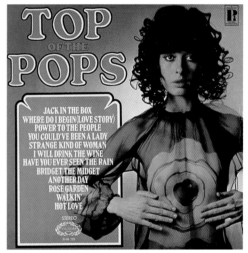

"Top of the morning to all you toe-tappers, tiny tots and Grand Pops. Yes, it's Top Of The Pops on top form! Sixteen fantastic, fabulous supersonic sounds - guaranteed to turn you around so need to get overwound! Again and again those talented Top Of The Poppers Band perform the latest tunes around. Whether rock, pop, disco or ska, you only need to look this far. Stock up fast, cos they ain't gonna last, Pickwick's remarkable coup. Top Of The Pops Volume 82." **Anon**

Artist Unoriginal Artists	**Artist** Unoriginal Artists	**Artist** Unoriginal Artists	**Artist** Unoriginal Artists	**Artist** Unoriginal Artists
Title Top Of The Pops	**Title** Top Of The Pops	**Title** Top Of The Pops	**Title** Top Of The Pops	**Title** Top Of The Pops
Record Label Hallmark/Pickwick UK	**Record Label** Hallmark/Pickwick UK	**Record Label** Hallmark/Pickwick UK	**Record Label** Hallmark/Pickwick UK	**Record Label** Hallmark/Pickwick UK
Date 1976	**Date** 1970	**Date** 1980	**Date** 1968	**Date** 1971
				Photography M. Laguens

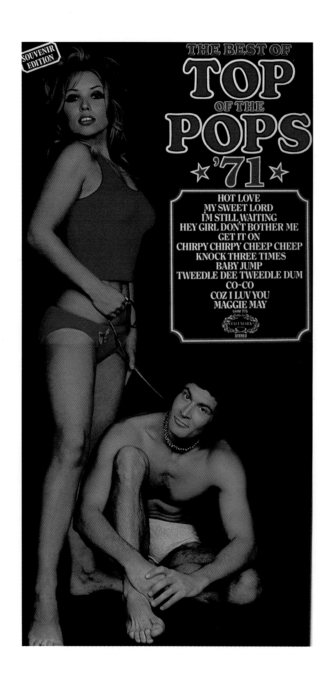

Artist *Unoriginal Artists*

Title *Top Of The Pops*

Record Label *Hallmark/Pickwick UK*

Date *1971*

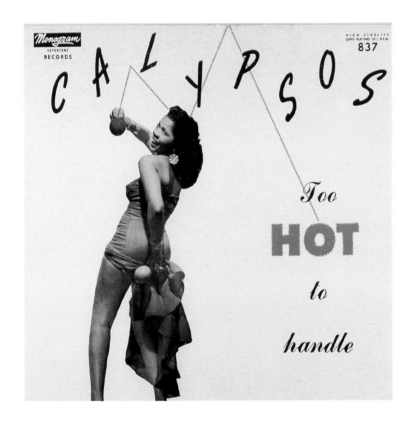

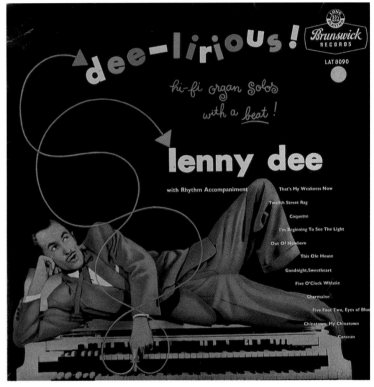

Artist Various

Title Calypsos, Too Hot To Handle

Record Label Monogram Records US

Artist Lenny Dee

Title Dee-Lirious

Record Label Brunswick UK

"Only the emotional depth of 101 strings can capture the contrasts of tender emotion and fiery crescendos of a night at gypsy campfires. Olive skinned girls, with flashing dark eyes, break the quite of night with the resounding rhythms of ribboned Tambourines.

The lovely rich tones of a violin fill the heart as it speaks of love that is old, new, lost, or yet to be discovered: for the music of the Gypsy speaks of a spirit that is restless, free and beautiful. Mystery and romance fill each shadow until the last fiery embers fade and all is darkness again." **Anon**

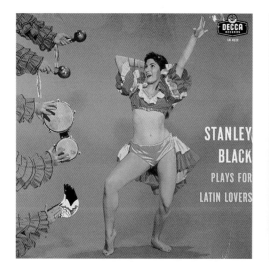

Artist Stanley Black

Title Stanley Black Plays For Latin Lovers

Record Label Decca UK

Date 1958

Artist Sonny Burke & His Orchestra

Title Let's Mambo

Record Label Brunswick/Decca UK

Date 1958

Artist 101 Strings

Title Gypsy Campfires

Record Label PYE Golden Guinea US

Date 1957

Artist The Curro Amaya Dancers

Title Flamenco

Record Label PYE Golden Guinea US

Artist Rogelio Y Su Orquesta

Featuring Johnny Conquet

Title Dance Rhythms Of Puerto Rico

Record Label Decca US

"A soft latin rhythm, rich romantic strings, a seductive piano, a lone horn and a beautiful soprano voice all mingle superbly, compelling you to dream of blue sunny skies, the moon with myriads of stars and the warmth of a latin love." **Anon**

Artist Noro Morales & His Orchestra
Title Latin Amercan Dance Party
Record Label Allegro Records UK
Date 1967

Artist Xavier Cugat
Title That Latin Beat
Record Label RCA UK
Date 1959

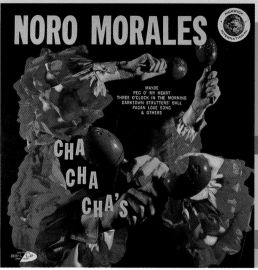

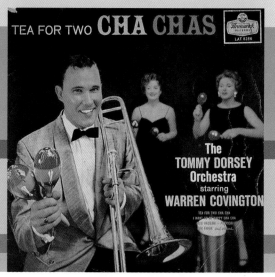

"The Cha-Cha-Cha is here and will stay for even the teenagers have accepted and love it. The split 4/4 time of the Cha Cha is infectious. Remember the tempo is "slow-slow-quick-quick-slow" and you're got it or repeat it as "slow-slow-cha-cha-cha" let these toe tingling rhythms get you and relax." **Anon**

Artist Pupi Campo & His Orchestra
Title 12 Cha-Chas & Merengues
Record Label Hollywood Records US

Artist Rene Hernandez Orchestra
Title Percussive Cha Cha Latino With Pacheco
Record Label Audio Fidelity US
Date 1962

Artist Noro Morales
Title Noro Morales Plays Cha Cha Cha's
Record Label Pickwick International UK

Artist The Tommy Dorsey Orchestra
Starring Warren Covington
Title Tea For Two Cha Cha's
Record Label Brunswick/Decca UK
Date 1958

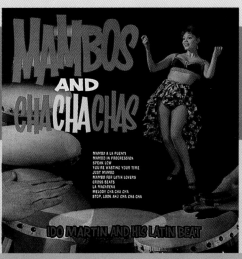

Artist Enoch Light & The Light Brigade

Title I Want To Be Happy Cha Cha's

Record Label Grand Award Record Corp US

Date 1960

Design Robert Stanley

Artist Ido Martin

Title Mambos & Cha Cha Cha's

Record Label ARC UK

Artist Tito Morano & His Orchestra

Title Lets Cha Cha Cha

Record Label PYE Golden Guinea UK

Date 1959

"In the background are the true sounds of hula dancing - the whisper of grass skirts, the ka-hea, or "call-out" of the lead hula dancer the deep beat of sharkskin drums, the crash of split-bamboo, the crisp sound of swirling red-and-yellow feathered rattles and rocks, and the thumping of gourds." **Webley Edwards**

Artist *The Surfmen*

Title *Hawaii*

Record Label *PYE Golden Guinea UK*

Date *1962*

Artist *Martin Denny*

Title *Quiet Village*

Record Label *London Records UK*

Date *1959*

Design *Pate/Francis & Associates*

Photography *Ivon Nagy*

Artist The Hawaii Calls Orchestra

Title Hula Island Favourites

Record Label Capitol US

Artist Johnny Pineapple & His Orchestra

Title Hawaiin Holiday

Record Label Allegro/Pickwick UK

Date 1965

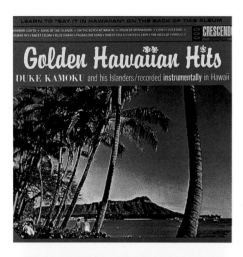

"The long, blue rollers of the Pacific curving their way toward sun-drenched beaches; cool lanais overlooking vast, neatly planned plantations; a festive luau, where the flames of torches seem to reflect the glittering of the stars overhead; and the ever present, sensuous music of the hula, that gracefully expressive dance which captures all the exotic beauty of the islands. The music of Hawaii is as natural as the lush vegetation and the flower-scented breezes. Guitars and Ukuleles play, and their softly insistent beat casts its spell. Primitive rhythms recall the glories of ancient Hawaii monarchs with mystical names; and the beautiful melodies distil a special blend of sentiment and nostalgia that haunts the memory." **Anon**

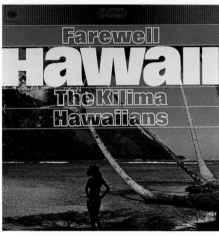

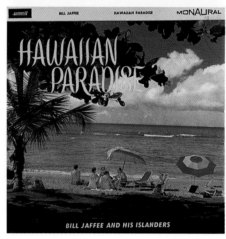

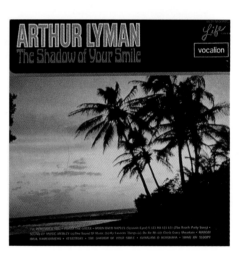

Artist Duke Kamoku & His Islanders

Title Golden Hawaiin Hits

Record Label Vogue Records UK

Date 1962

Artist The Waikiki Beach Boys

Title South Sea Island Magic

Record Label MFP/EMI UK

Date 1966

Photography PAF International

Artist The Kilima Hawaiins

Title Farewell Hawaii

Record Label CBS US

Photography Galaxy

Artist Bill Jaffee & His Islanders

Title Hawaiian Paradise

Record Label Summitt US

Photography Picturepoint

Artist Arhtur Lyman

Title The Shadow Of Your Smile

Record Label Vogue/Decca UK

Date 1967

Design Edwin Francis

Photography Muriel Matson

Artist Rudi Wairata & His Mena
Moeria Minstrels
Title Waikiki Welcome
Record Label Gemeni UK
Date 1965

Artist The Rio Carnival Orchestra
Title Honeymoon In South America
Record Label Miller US
Date 1958

Artist Arthur Lyman

Title Taboo

Record Label Vogue Records UK

Date 1959

Photography Werner Stoy

Artist Arthur Lyman

Title Yellow Bird

Record Label Vogue Records/Decca UK

Date 1959

Design George Liberman

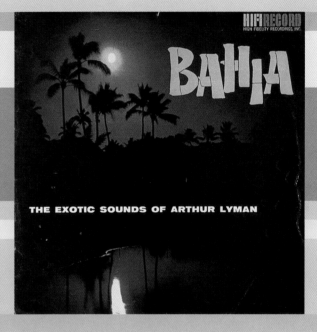

Artist Arthur Lyman

Title Hawaiian Sunset

Record Label Vogue Records UK

Date 1959

Artist Arthur Lyman

Title Bahia

Record Label Vogue Records UK

Date 1959

Artist Steven Smith & Father

Title Steven Smith & Father & Sixteen
Great Songs

Record Label Decca UK

Date 1972

Artist The Eric Delaney Band

Title Skin Ed Goes Skin Deep

Record Label Norwood Records UK

Date 1980

Artist The Peddlers

Title The Fantastic Peddlers

Record Label Fontana UK

Date 1967

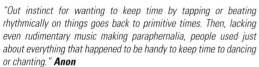

"Out instinct for wanting to keep time by tapping or beating rhythmically on things goes back to primitive times. Then, lacking even rudimentary music making paraphernalia, people used just about everything that happened to be handy to keep time to dancing or chanting." **Anon**

Artist Harry Breuer & His Quintet
Title Mallet Magic
Record Label Audio Fidelity UK
Date 1958
Photography Bob Witt

Artist Ted Heath & His Orchestra
Title Ted Heath Goes Latin
Record Label Decca UK
Date 1961

Artist Dick Schory's New Percussion Ensemble
Title Music For Bang Baa-room & Harp
Record Label RCA UK
Date 1958

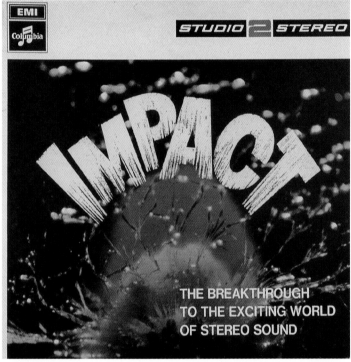

"Melody is only one of the several ingredients that go to make music. It is certainly the element which is easiest of apreciation, but even in the shortest and simplest of compositions harmony is equelly necessary, and interest can be greatly enhanced by the appropriate choice of instrumental colour." **W.A. Chislett**

Artist Original Sound Recording

Title Off Beat Sound Effects

Record Label BBC Records

Date 1975

Photography Adrian Davies, Paul Hyett & Nigel Grigg

Artist Various

Title Impact

Record Label Columbia/EMI

Date 1968

Photography Royal Aircraft Establishment

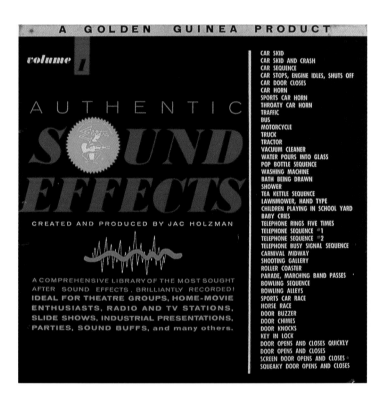

Artist Jac Holzman

Title Authentic Sound Effects

Record Label PYE Golden Guinea UK

Artist Various

Title High Fidelity Test Record

Record Label Gramaphone Record Review US

"Included in the astounding array of percussions heard are Congos, Bongos, Tymball, Cocktail Drums, Boobams, Cowbell, Ass's Jaw, Conch Shell and Guido, as well as the more ordinary percussions, such as Tambourine Snare Drums, Wood Block, Cymbals, Chinese Gong and Sleigh Bells." **Anon**

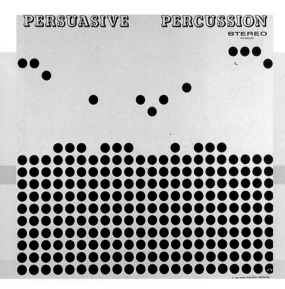

Artist Enoch Light & The Light Brigade	**Artist** Original Sound Recording	**Artist** Terry Snyder & The All Stars
Title Provocative Percussion	**Title** An Audio Obstacle Course Era III	**Title** Persuasive Percussion
Record Label Command Records US	**Record Label** Shure US	**Record Label** Command Records US
Date 1959	**Date** 1973	**Date** 1959
Design Josef Albers		**Design** Josef Albers

"Stereo action is a revolutionary concept of stereo recording in which instruments, singers, whole sections, and even full orchestras are placed into movement so that the listener has, literally, music his eyes can follow."

"Stereo action is a conscious and deliberate effort to set music in motion by utilizing actual movement of instruments and sounds from one speaker to the other, and even at times, suspending an instrument or sound between speakers. It is a pioneering concept in stereo listening, and resulted from years of extensive experiments and remarkable technical breakthroughs." **Anon**

Artist Ferrante & Teicher
Title The Dynamic Twin Pianos Of Ferrante & Teicher
Record Label London Records UK
Date 1960

Artist Original Sound Recording
Title Stereophonic Demonstration Test Record
Record Label EMI UK
Date 1962

Artist Original Sound Recording
Title Stereo Spectacular Demonstration & Sound Effects
Record Label Audio Fidelity US

WILD STRINGS
Werner Müller and his Orchestra

eclips

19'11

Fidelio   GUITARS ON FIRE   NICK NANTOS & HIS FIREBALLERS   MONAURAL

Guitars on Fire

"The classics get their comeuppance and the pops rule the roost in this lively pot-pourri of musical favourites - a savoury platter of tunes light and listenable, spiced with lively harmonies, and served with a full measure of orchestral sparkle." **Robert Sherman**

Artist Werner Muller & His Orchestra	**Artist** Nick Nantos & His Fireballers
Title Wild Strings	**Title** Guitars On Fire
Record Label Decca UK	**Record Label** Fidelio UK
Date 1969	**Date** 1964
Photography David Wedgbury	**Photography** Picturepoint

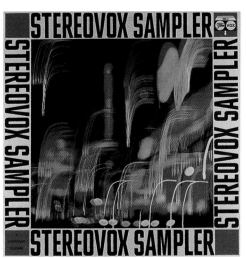

"The aim of this record is to provide a means for the demanding listener to check record playing equipment without the need for expensive and complicated instruments. With care it can remain a lasting tool, the standard of which will not change with time, whereas the equipment itself - and indeed the human ear - must certainly alter with age." **Anon**

Artist Original Sound Recording	**Artist** Original Sound Recording	**Artist** Jean Jacques Perry &	**Artist** Original Sound Recording
Title Sounds Out Of This World	**Title** Stereovox Sampler	Gershon Kingsley	**Title** How To Give Yourself A Stereo Check Out
Record Label Omega US	**Record Label** Vox US	**Title** The In Sound From Way Out	**Record Label** Decca UK
Design Leon McFadden	**Date** 1958	**Record Label** Vanguard US	**Date** 1967
Photography Gian Greguoli	**Photography** Sid Kaplan	**Date** 1965	
		Design Jules Halfant	

"I have treated each sound as if it were a piece of music in itself. For me, every sound has it's own minute form - is composed of small flashing rhythms, shifting tones, has momentum, comes, vanishes, lives out it's own structure, and since we are used to hearing sounds together, either, juxtapsed or compered, one sound alone seems simple - but so are the round scruffed stones lying about everywhere, until you crack one apart and all it's intricate beauty takes you by surprise." **Anna Lockwood**

Artist Anna Lockwood
Title Glass World Of Anna Lockwood
Record Label Tangent UK
Date 1970
Design Robert Morgan
Photography John Goldblatt

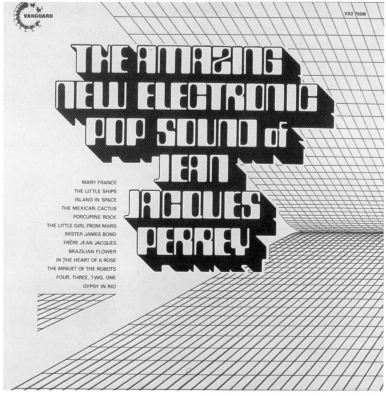

"Popular music from electronic instruments is what this programme offers for the joy of the present and a glimpse of the future. This is the age of electronics. Every day brings evidence of the incredible calculations and fantastic jobs electronics can do. Why should it not also add to the pleaures of life? Why should not its immense possiblities for new spectrums of sound help inspire our music? By our music I mean popular music, which is a genuine art form and means of expression with its own strength and legitimacy." **Jean Jacques Perry**

Artist Buddy Cole

Title Ingenuity In Sound

Record Label Warner Brothers US

Date 1962

Artist Jean Jacques Perrey

Title The Amazing New Electronic Pop Sound
Of Jean Jacques Perrey

Record Label Vanguard/RCA UK

Date 1972

Artist Various	**Artist** Various	**Artist** Various	**Artist** Various	**Artist** Various
Title Hi Fi Stereo Festival	**Title** Love Songs In Hi Fi Stereo	**Title** Big Band In Hi Fi Stereo	**Title** Golden Instrumentals In Hi Fi Stereo	**Title** Happy South America Hi Fi Stereo
Record Label Polydor UK	**Record Label** Polydor UK	**Record Label** Polydor UK	**Record Label** Polydor UK	**Record Label** Polydor UK
Date 1973	**Date** 1973	**Date** 1973	**Date** 1973	**Date** 1973
Design Motivation Techniques Ltd	**Design** Motivation Techniques Ltd	**Design** Motivation Techniques Ltd	**Design** Motivation Techniques Ltd	**Design** Motivation Techniques Ltd
Photography Motivation Techniques Ltd	**Photography** Motivation Techniques Ltd	**Photography** Motivation Techniques Ltd	**Photography** Motivation Techniques Ltd	**Photography** Motivation Techniques Ltd

"14 sound spectaculars - each track a unique experience in sound, specially chosen for the thrill of listening. A thrill that has placed Phase 4 Stereo firmly at the top; a position maintained through constant pioneering of the latest technological innovations. The 14 numbers on this record demonstrate the success that Decca's engineers have achieved, and the overall effect of utilising individual detail unapproached by conventional disc standards. Everything is in phase 4 Stereo - orchestras, vocal groups, big bands, marching bands and Latin bands. Music from around the world, from stage and screen, from waltzes to Rock 'n' Roll, not forgetting the concert series of familiar classics and the many sound effect spectaculars." **Tony D'amato**

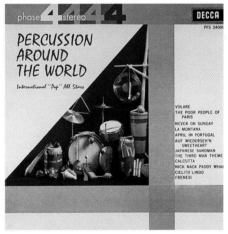

Artist Edmundo Ross & His Orchestra

Title Hair Goes Latin

Record Label Decca UK

Date 1970

Design Marvin Edson Associates

Photography Photo Media Ltd

Artist Roger Laredo & His Orchestra

Title Italy

Record Label Decca UK

Date 1962

Artist International Pop All Stars

Title Percussion Around The World

Record Label Decca UK

Date 1962

Artist Edmundo Ros & His Orchestra

Title Latin Hits I Missed

Record Label Decca UK

Date 1967

"This album does more than just hold a selection of tunes denoting far-away places. It attempts to capture not only the colour of a locale - which is done with a judicious use of the instrumentation - but it attempts realisticly to excite the spirit native, to the place from which the song originates.

As you follow these sounds around the globe, you will feel the special magic of this album. You will feel the rooftops of Paris, the cool shade of German Woods, the sun of Italy, the bustling activity of a street in India, the warmth of a Latin night. It's record making at it's best and it's the best sound on records, remarkably and faithfully reproduced." **Anon**

Artist Klaus Wunderlich
Title Around The World With Klaus Wunderlich
Record Label Teldec Germany

Artist The Dave Brubeck Quartet
Title Jazz Impressions Of Eurasia
Record Label Fontana UK
Date 1958
Photography Bob Willoughby

Artist Duffy Ravenscroft & His Orchestra
Title Jet Ride
Record Label Gallotone South Africa
Date 1953

"Listen to the many moods on this album. The haunting sounds, from India, of the Sitar . . . the warmth of the trumpet . . . the heart of a harmonica. Add the romance of strings and voices and be lulled into a sense of international love." **Ivor Raymonde**

Artist El Al Israel In Flight Entertainment Program
Title Hava Nagila Festival Vol 2
Record Label CBS Israel
Date 1974

Artist El Al Israel In Flight Entertainment Program
Title Hava Nagila Festival
Record Label CBS Israel
Date 1973

Artist Various With Bobby Richards & His Orchestra
Title From Europe With Love
Record Label The World Record Club Ltd UK
Date 1965
Design Peter Gammond

"There are countless ways to soak up the sounds and pleasures of London, by common consensus and royal, probably the most exciting city in today's world. You can make the rounds by bus or Rolls Royce, by day or night and find yourself charmed; inundated by the Mod or the mad, by the native or naive. Whatever your choice of carrier, the tempo, the harmony, the motion will never strike you as dull." **Moort Goode**

Artist The First Impression & The Good Earth

Title Swinging London

Record Label Saga Records UK

Date 1968

Artist Band Of The Grenadier Guards

Title Holiday In England

Record Label Decca UK

Date 1958

Photography Betram Follett

"Paris - glittering, sparkling queen of the Seine, home of laughter, gayety and romance, city of a thousand dreams, a thousand delights. The accordions of Paris are her voice and her song, telling of the hopes, loves and desires of her people. Caught in a magic web of melody are all the varied flavours, exciting emotions and thrilling experiences that go to make up this beloved city." **Anon**

Artist Pierre Simone
Title Bistro
Record Label Allegro Records UK
Date 1968

Artist Jo Basile His Accordian & Orchestra
Title Accordion De Paris
Record Label Audio Fidelity Ltd UK
Date 1960
Photography Bob Witt

Artist The Esso Trinidad Steelband

Title The Esso Trinidad Steelband On Tour

Record Label ARC Sound Ltd US

Date 1967

Artist The Silvertone Steel Orchestra

Title The Silvertone Steel Orchestra

Record Label Joy Records UK

Date 1971

Artist Amral's Gay Flamingoes

Title Carnival In Trinidad

Date 1968

Design Compton Welch

Photography Oswald Berkley

Artist The Trinidad Steel Band

Title The Original Trinidad Steel Band

Record Label Polydor UK

Design Paragon Publicity

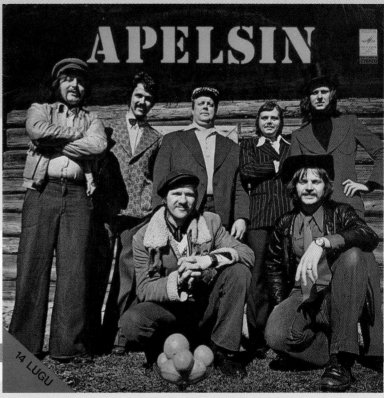

Artist Luis Alberto Del Parana

Title Best Of Trio Los Paraguayos

Record Label Fontana UK

Date 1957

Artist Apelsin

Title Apelsin

Record Label Meloodia USSR

Date 1979

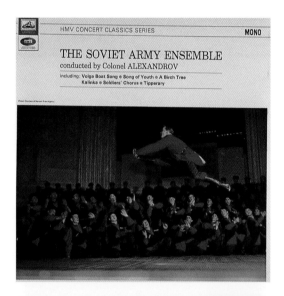

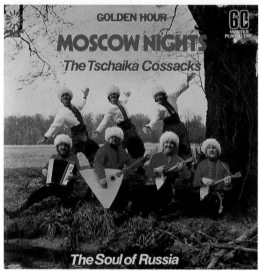

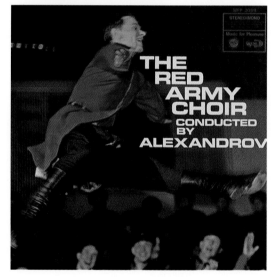

Artist The Soviet Army Ensemble

Title The Soviet Army Ensemble

Record Label EMI UK

Date 1956

Artist Sasha Palinoff & His Russian

Gypsy Orchestra

Title Fastest Balaika In The West

Record Label PYE Golden Guinea UK

Date 1964

Artist The Tschaika Cossacks

Title The Soul Of Russia

Record Label Golden Hour UK

Date 1974

Artist The Red Army Choir

Title The Red Army Choir

Record Label EMI/Music For Pleasure

Design Jan Wiltshire

Photography Novosti Press Agency

"And so they came, these songs from foreign lands, and mingled with our own and the current American hits, and became just as much a part of our lives as the songs that spoke our own language. They spoke an international language of good melody and the timeless poetry of love." **Anon**

Artist Various
Title Holiday In Italy
Record Label EMI UK
Date 1959
Photography Italian Tourist Board

Artist Manual & The Music Of The Mountains
Title Mardi Gras
Record Label Columbia/EMI UK
Date 1972

Artist Various
Title From Israel With Love
Record Label Hed-Arzi Ltd Israel
Date 1972
Photography Norbert

Artist Various
Title Israel
Record Label Phillips France
Date 1964
Photography Paris Match/Litran Courrier

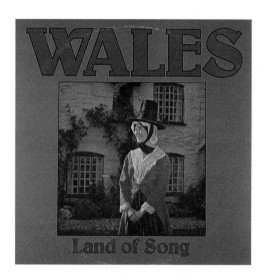

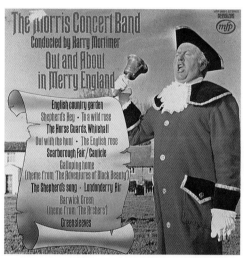

Artist The Newport Male Voice Choir

Title Wales Land Of Song

Record Label Stereo Gold Award UK

Date 1974

Artist The Morris Concert Band

Title Out And About In Merry England

Record Label MFP/EMI UK

Date 1975

Design Ross J. Waters

Photography Terry Beard

Artist Neil Linden & The Highlanders

Title The Pride Of Scotland

Record Label Marble Arch/PYE UK

Artist Quincy Jones Big Band

Title Travellin

Record Label Mercury UK

Photography B. Mulder

Artist Various

Title Super Stereo Sound Sampler

Record Label Mercury UK

Artist *Rawicz & Landauer*
Title *South American Hits*
Record Label *Wing/Phillips UK*
Date *1959*

Artist Acker Bilk

Title Call Me Mister

Record Label EMI UK

Date 1963

Design Peter Leslie

Photography Patrick Gwynn-Jones

Artist Earl Grant

Title Fly Me To The Moon

Record Label Brunswick/Decca UK

Date 1963

Photography Hal Buksbaum

Artist *Troll*

Title *Troll Turned To Stone*

Record Label *Intersound Germany*

Photography *Intersound*

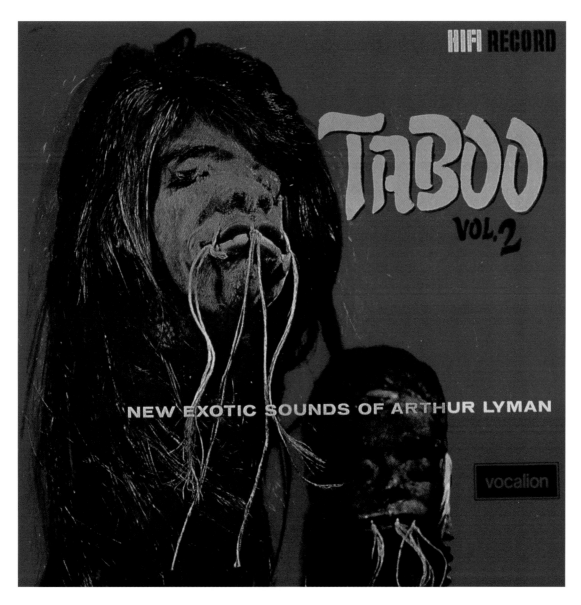

"Drums almost burst out of the loudspeakers; voices and guitars are fused in a glorious, full-throated sound; and the walls of your room seem ablaze with wild, throbbing rhythmic patterns from a wide variety of percussion instruments. This is Voodoo music-exotic, mysterious, unhinhibited, sometimes frantic, and sometimes soothing." **James Wynn**

Artist Arthur Lyman
Title Taboo Vol 2
Record Label Vogue/Decca UK
Date 1968

Artist Manuel & The Music Of The Mountains

Title Mardi Gras

Record Label Columbia/EMI UK

Date 1960

Artist Hans Kary

Title Hare Krishna

Record Label Hare Krsna Records Germany

Date 1974

Artist The Mexical Singers

Title The Unique Vocal Instrumentalizations Of
The Mexical Singers

Date 1966

Record Label Warner Bros US

Design Ed Thrasher

Artist Al Caiola
Title Tuff Guitar Tijuana Style
Record Label United Artists/EMI UK
Date 1966

"A flip of the disc places you in the midst of the pulsating, brooding, yet heart - quickening African jungle. You close your eyes and listen to the bird-calls, the strange sounds in the jungle night." **Anon**

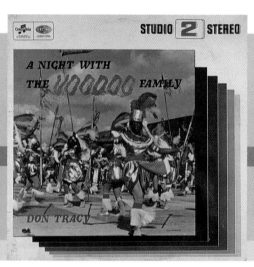

Artist Mighty Sheller & Lord Hawk

Title Sheller & Hawk

Record Label Soufriere Trinidad

Date 1973

Artist Chaino & His African Percussion Safari

Title Jungle Echos

Record Label Mecca/Egmont UK

Design Leon McFadden

Photography George Pickow

Artist Don Tracy

Title A Night With The Voodoo Family

Record Label EMI UK

Artist Harry Belafonte & The Islanders

Title Caribbean

Record Label The World Record Club Ltd UK

"Music is a whip and men are slaves groaning in a spasm of
vibrant toil, Dynamic Calypso." **Shake Keane**

Artist Meat Heat
Title Ultra Funk
Record Label Contempo UK

Artist Lyra De Xopoto
Title Lembrancas Do Carnaval Carioca
Record Label Companhia Brasileira De Discos Brasil
Photography Van Erven

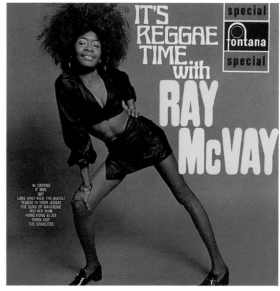

Artist Various

Title Hair

Record Label Hallmark/Pickwick UK

Artist Ray McVay & His Orchestra

Title It's Reggae Time With Ray McVay

Record Label Fontana UK

Date 1970

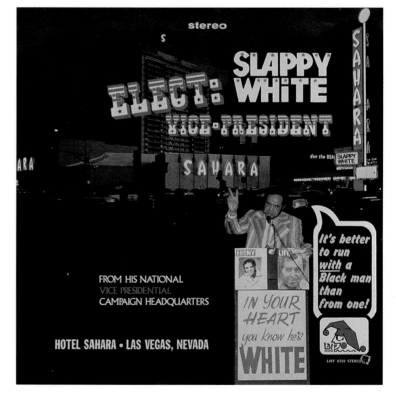

Artist Skillet & Leroy

Title The Goodly Soul

Record Label Laff US

Design Howard Goldstein

Photography Dominic Belmonte

Artist Slappy White

Title Elect Slappy White Vice President

Record Label Laff US

"The history of the guitar is very old. Man learnt in his primitive days that a plucked string made a pleasant sound and through the ages, from the days of the troubadours to our own, the guitar, has been the basic instrument of popular song in many countries. Even the owl, when he went to sea in a beautiful pea-green boat looked up to the stars above and sang to a small guitar." **Anon**

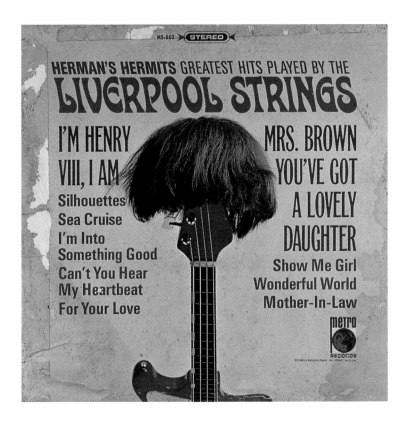

Artist *The Liverpool Strings*

Title *Herman's Hermits Greatest Hits*

Record Label *MGM Records US*

Photography *Sigred Owen*

Artist *The 50 Guitars Of Tommy Garrett*

Title *50 Guitars Visist Hawaii*

Record Label *Liberty/EMI UK*

Date *1962*

Photography *Studio Five*

Percolator
Tequila
Slag Solution
Wheels
und viele andere

musicor
STEREO

More
HOT
Butter

Artist Various

Title More Hot Butter

Record Label Musicor Germany

Artist Rice & Beans Orchestra

Title Rice & Beans

Record Label Contempo UK

Date 1977

Design John Kittavadick

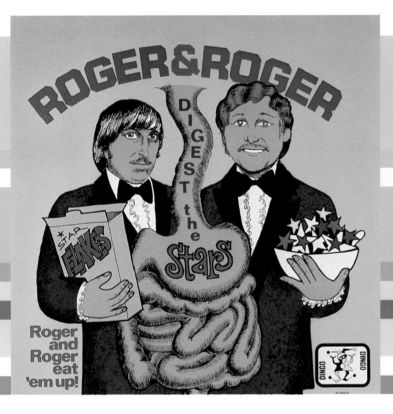

Artist Roger & Roger

Title Roger & Roger Digest The Stars

Record Label Dingo Records US

Artist Geoff Muldaur & Amos Garrett

Record Label Flying Fish Records US

Date 1978

Design Laura Karp

Illustration Yasuo Yagi

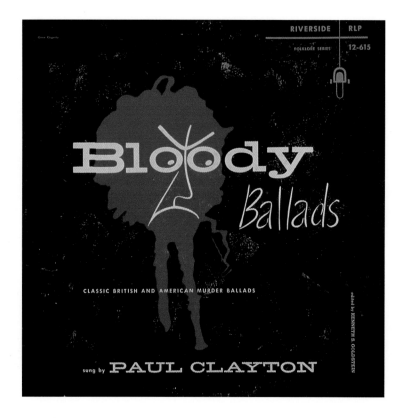

Artist Paul Clayton

Title Bloody Ballads

Record Label Riverside Records US

Date 1956

Artist James Last

Title Hair

Record Label Polydor UK

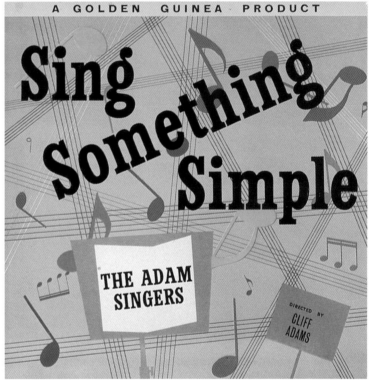

Artist The Electratones

Title Guitar Bossa Nova

Record Label Gone Latin US

Design Moskof Morrison Inc

Artist The Adam Singers & Orchestra

Title Sing Something Simple

Record Label PYE/Golden Guinea UK

Date 1959

"Any time the pressures on earth get a little too strong and enervating for you, use this album as a ticket to a trip above the clouds, away from all worldly cares and worries. Just sit back, relax and let others worry about trips to the moon." **Bernie Green**

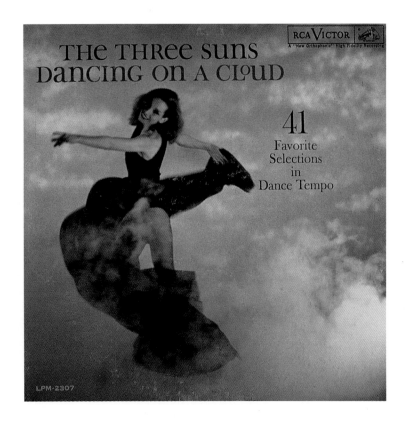

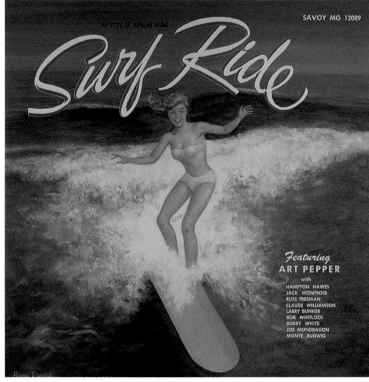

Artist The Three Suns

Title Dancing On A Cloud

Record Label RCA Victor UK

Date 1961

Artist Art Pepper & His Groups

Title Surf Ride

Record Label Savoy Records Inc US

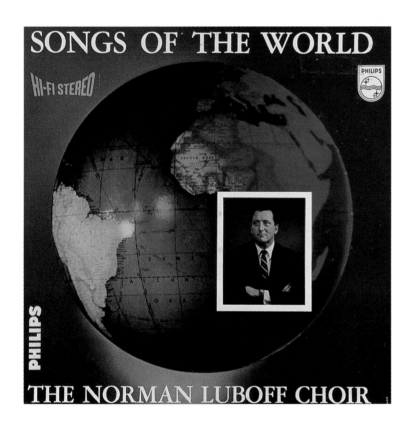

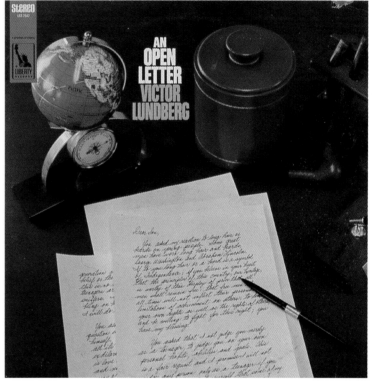

Artist The Norman Luboff Choir

Title Songs Of The World

Record Label Phillips UK

Artist Victor Lundberg

Title An Open Letter

Record Label Liberty US

Photography Woody Woodward

Artist Peter Sellers

Title Songs For Swingin Sellers

Record Label Parlophone/EMI UK

Date 1959

Photography Ken Palmer